Escape from Islam

HASS HIRJI-WALJI
& JARYL STRONG

Tyndale House
Publishers, Inc.
Wheaton, Illinois

To my wife Kathy

Scripture quotations, unless
otherwise noted, are from the
New International Version
(NIV), © 1978 by New York
International Bible Society.
Other versions cited are the
New American Standard Bible
(NASB), © 1960, 1962, 1963,
1968, 1971 by The Lockman
Foundation, La Habra,
California; and *The Living
Bible* (TLB), © 1961 by
Tyndale House Publishers.
Quotations from the Quran are
cited from *The Koran
Interpreted* by Arthur J. Arberry
(New York: Macmillan, 1964).

Library of Congress Catalog
Card Number 80-54493
ISBN 0-8423-0712-5, paper
Copyright © 1981 by
Hassanain Hirji-Walji and Jaryl
Strong. All rights reserved.
First printing, April 1981.
Printed in the United States
of America.

Acknowledgement

The authors and publisher
are grateful to Jan Markell
for her help
in the early stages of this book.

CONTENTS

Preface 7

One **Uganda** 11

Two **My Islamic Roots** 17

Three **Amin** 21

Four **Blood Bath** 27

Five **Big Daddy or Big Dummy?** 33

Six **Flight from Uganda** 43

Seven **America** 49

Eight **Campus Life** 55

Nine **Scream in the Dark** 63

Ten **The Living End** 69

Eleven **Surprised by Joy** 85

Twelve **Aftermath** 101

Thirteen **Fullness of Life** 111

Fourteen **Truth** 119

Notes 141

PREFACE

Islam has caught the attention of the world. The revolution
in Iran, the continuing hotbed of Middle East diplomacy,
the oil wealth of the OPEC nations, Muslim militancy in
African politics, and the Iranian hostage crisis all have
played their role in the resurgence of Islam in recent times.
An estimated 750 million Muslims now bow toward Mecca
daily—about one-sixth of the world's population. Islam has
gained a recognition in world affairs today that it has not
received for centuries—but not without its disparaging
incidents.

Perhaps one of the most notorious of recent events
associated with the world of Islam was in 1971, when a
professed Muslim led a successful military coup that over-
threw the government of Uganda. It was a time of rejoicing
for the country's Muslims, for Idi Amin Dada, who later
proclaimed himself President for Life, promised to make
Uganda an Islamic country, despite its Christian majority.
Claiming visions from God, Amin began to purge the
country of all those suspected of being a possible threat to
his regime. Christians and political opponents of all kinds
were slaughtered by the thousands.

Since my family and I were devout Muslims, we never

thought that we would be in any danger from Amin. However, within two years we realized how deceived we had been, for even Muslims began to come under persecution if they were Asian descendants.

My forefathers came from India in the 1880s to help build a railroad. Like most of the nineteenth-century immigrants from Asia, my grandparents then stayed in Uganda, their children and grandchildren becoming the shopkeepers and merchants of the country. But in 1972, "Big Daddy" Amin, believing the Asians had a stranglehold on Uganda's economy, gave all Asians only a few weeks in which to flee the country. He later changed his edict to include only those Asians who could not prove their Ugandan citizenship. But every Asian knew that if he did not leave the country soon he was assured of almost certain death at the hands of Amin's henchmen.

During the three-month period preceding our escape from Uganda, bullets from Amin's soldiers penetrated the bodies of many Asians. My family and I prayed continually for Allah's protection. For days we searched for information about a country somewhere that would open its doors to us. Finally, when we received word that the United States was accepting two thousand Asians, we quickly availed ourselves of the opportunity to come to this tremendous land of freedom.

In America I found not only refuge from the brutality of Amin, but greater still, salvation in Christ. Before coming to the United States I knew little about the Bible and the Christian faith. Islam was all I knew. But in Christ I have found the answer to the deeper aspirations and longings of my life which Islam left unfulfilled.

It has been several years now since I left Uganda, and my heart is still burdened for my homeland. Although Amin was ousted from power by Tanzanian troops early in 1979, Uganda remains in chaos. The outlook for the immediate future looks bleak. We must pray for the welfare and recovery of Uganda and its suffering people. May God grant the many Christians there the necessary courage and wisdom to lead the country out of its devastation and into spiritual, political, and economic stability.

Meanwhile, justice has not come to Idi Amin. The deposed dictator is reported to be dwelling securely within the borders of either Libya or Saudia Arabia.[1] Still not one to withhold his opinions, foolish though they may be, Amin, reflecting on the prospects for world peace, has offered this solution: "I propose getting rid of conventional armaments and replacing them with reasonably priced atomic and hydrogen bombs that would be distributed equally throughout the world. Only when one nation fears another can mutual respect between nations be truly attained."[2] Such a statement (made since his exile) reveals the demented mind of the mercurial and impetuous tyrant who brought Uganda to the brink of complete ruin.

This book is written as a testimony to the magnificent love and grace of God which he has so mercifully displayed in my life. Let it never be interpreted as an affront to Islam. I love the Muslim peoples of the world. My purpose is to exalt and glorify the Lord Jesus Christ. I can serve no other —for in him I have found the Truth.

—*Hassanain Hirji-Walji*

Note: Some names of family members have been changed to protect their anonymity.

ONE
UGANDA

It was a cool spring day in April, three days after I had given
my life to Christ. Now I was alone walking down a
Minneapolis sidewalk, without a coat, and with two dimes in
my pocket. I had just been expelled from my home.

"As long as you've found your own God, find your own
place," my oldest brother yelled at me as I walked out the
door. Upon hearing that I had become a Christian, he
had begun shaking and hitting me, as if he were trying to
bring me back to my senses for denying Islam. Deeply
grieved, yet angered, he was weeping frantically because of
my newfound allegiance to Christ.

Once outside the door, I glanced behind me in response
to my family's weeping. Oblivious to what was before
me, I found myself tumbling down the front steps. But the
pain of my body meeting the concrete was not as severe
as the pain of hearing my mother's desperate scream when
she learned of my having turned to Christ. Frustrated
and brokenhearted at the loss of my family, I exclaimed,
"Well, Jesus, is this what I get for accepting you?"

Often things do not happen the way we plan them. When
my family fled Uganda in 1972, I had intended to win the

American friends I would make to the Muslim faith. But now, having left Islam in favor of Christianity, I was disowned by my own family.

Life in my childhood had been quiet. I loved Uganda, the land Winston Churchill called the "Pearl of Africa." The land stands unsurpassed in sheer natural beauty. The air is pure, the forests unfold a magnificent variety of luscious green foliage, and the vast plains teem with an abundance of wildlife. Murchison Falls (now Kabalega Falls) is an awesome sight as it produces the thunderous roar marking the beginning of the Nile River's long northward journey to the Mediterranean. I loved to gaze upon the Ruwenzori Mountains, whose snow-capped peaks are often shrouded in clouds.

At that time, bustling Kampala—a clean and prosperous city by African standards—bloomed almost year-round with the beauty and fragrance of banana and mango trees and an abundance of flowers. The Asians, many of whom were descendants of the Indians who had come by British colonial government invitation in the 1880s to build "the iron snake," had become the owners and operators of most of Kampala's attractive little shops. And some, like my father, had tilled fertile Ugandan soil.

Due in part to the Asian influence, Uganda had become one of the more prosperous African countries. Yet deep poverty was the plight of many native Ugandans. I remember the rows of mud and wattle huts on the edge of our city. Blacks there might earn no more in a week than what they got from the sale of a pineapple or a tomato. Eventually the existence of such poverty alongside the comparatively wealthier Asian community prompted Idi Amin to turn on us.

In 1971 the shadow of one of the world's most outrageous rulers began to cover the land, taking us all by surprise. The carefree years of my youth were to come to an end. By the time I reached the age of sixteen, the land flowed with the blood of innocent Africans and Asians.

As a child I knew that Uganda was ruled by Britain through the *Kabaka,* the tribal king of the Buganda tribe. Of the thirty-nine tribes throughout the country, the Buganda was the largest, most prosperous, and best educated. When Uganda achieved independence from Britain in 1962, the *Kabaka,* King Freddie (Sir Edward Frederick Mutesa II), became our president. Four years later, however, Apolo Milton Obote, our prime minister, ousted King Freddie, sending him into exile. Attempting to unify the country, Obote abolished the four tribal kingdoms and suspended the constitution. But the new president's tightfisted rule was to lead to his political demise. While Obote was out of the country, General Idi Amin, commander of the Army, stormed King Freddie's former palace in Kampala and established himself as president.

My family, well known to the Muslin community in Kampala, was very devout in its adherence to the beliefs and practices of Islam. As Muslims, we lived by the law of Allah,[1] and we observed the teachings of our holy book, the Quran (Koran). Our lives centered around pleasing Allah through prayer, fasting, and performing good deeds. We had very strict laws governing our worship and fasting. For example, during the month-long Fast of Ramadan, there are even rules about how one should swallow saliva.

The commitment to Islamic principles tends to unite the Muslim family into a very cohesive unit. In fact, many Muslim families are so closely knit together that the parents arrange the marriages of their children through mutual consent with another Muslim family. After marriage, the newlyweds often take up residence with the husband's family. Had I continued a Muslim, I too would have had a marriage arranged for me, and undoubtedly would have led a quiet, American life with the rest of my family. But my life was to change drastically in the coming years.

As an electrician, my father worked long, tiring hours. In addition to this, he was the head cook of Kampala's *mosque* (the Muslim's place of public worship, similar to a Christian church or chapel). For the work he did at the mosque he wanted no money. This work was done out of a great love for Allah.

My father's income was barely enough to support our family. Most of his money went for food, and all of my mother's time went to caring for the household. I had three brothers—Mohammed, Hassen, and Hanif; and one sister —Zehra; and we seven became only a small part of the household. Also living under our roof was my grandmother and my uncle and his family, making a total of sixteen staying in our small Ugandan home. Often other relatives would move in with us for a month or two at a time, resulting in as many as fifty people being packed into our little house. It was my father's responsibility to feed us all.

But this is the preferred life-style of many Muslim families. It is the height of our joy to be surrounded by other family members. There is no such word as inconvenience. Often so many people slept on the floor of our home that we could not walk about the house at night without stepping on some of them.

By American standards our home was a paradox. My father's income was scant, yet we had a servant. Almost every Asian family employed a native Ugandan servant, for the amount of his wages was only a few cents per day. These servants and their families usually lived in huts near the homes of their employers. Unfortunately, many Ugandans could make a living only by begging from door to door. In Kampala, each Friday was the official day during which beggars could solicit from house to house. Often as many as one hundred came to our home on a Friday, each receiving about fifteen cents and some bread. We always gave the money cheerfully, but only to those who were disabled, and therefore unable to work. Besides, as Muslims, we were taught that any beggar might be an angel from God.

Since practically all of our money went for food, our

expenditures for clothing, medicine, and household items were few. We just had to do without, except for the essentials. Though we lacked material prosperity, we had a deeper, richer, more abiding wealth; namely, a special sense of family unity and a sincere love for one another.

TWO
MY ISLAMIC ROOTS

My uncle had once predicted that I would someday be a Muslim minister. I had an insatiable desire to learn the Quran and to be a devout Muslim. Almost as soon as I began to learn my native tongue, I was being taught Arabic so that someday I would be able to read the Quran in its original language. By the age of five, I began to fast for the month of Ramadan, during which Muslims can eat only after sunset. My life was so saturated with Islam that I was barely aware that other religions existed in the world. I prayed toward Mecca five times a day: once before sunrise, again at noon, then at 2:00 P.M., before sunset, and finally once more after sunset. As a child I faithfully attended all prayer meetings and Quran studies.

Next to my love for Allah and Islam, my father was my life. I often pretended to be sick so that I might skip school and spend days with him. I was frequently at his side as he cooked in the mosque. As a result of the many days I spent with him, observing him at work on electrical applicances, I too wanted to become an electrician like him.

But when I was ten, Father became very ill with diabetes. I never left his side during his final days of sickness. He closed his eyes at 2:00 A.M. one frightfully dark night—at the precise time he told us he would die. That night I remained at his side until morning. I was heartstruck at my father's death and desired more than ever to be an electrician like him when I grew up.

After our father's death, Mohammed, my oldest brother, had to take over the financial responsibility for our family. At a tourist hotel in Kampala he earned about $100 a month. In addition to this, Mohammed was still enrolled in secondary school, so when he came home from the hotel at 1:00 A.M., he would study in preparation for his early morning classes. Since this was obviously too much of a strain, he had to drop out of school and work full time to support the family.

Mohammed was very active in preaching and in reciting the Quran in public, enhancing our reputation as one of the more devout Muslim families in Kampala. I had now read through the Quran nine times and had memorized many chapters. Like most Muslims whose native language is not Arabic, I had learned only how to properly pronounce the words of our Scriptures without actually understanding what I was "reading." But nevertheless there was a certain mystique in reciting the Quran in Arabic, for I believed, as do all Muslims, that the very words of the Quran were handed down from God. Just speaking the words, so I thought, brought a special closeness to God.

Although I was only ten, I entered a contest at which many Muslim teenagers competed in a Quran quiz. The contestants totaled around four hundred young people, some of whom were children of Muslim clergymen. To my surprise, as well as to the others', I took third place. I would continue to be exercised on my knowledge of the Quran, as my sister and I would often quiz each other on our Holy Book.

Two years later I went to a minister to study Urdu, a language used in many Muslim books and prayers. Because I was so young, the clergyman looked at me skeptically as I asked him to teach me Urdu. He asked me to read from the Quran. When I read the passages perfectly he not only agreed to teach me Urdu, he also made me an assistant of his Quran class.

I entered secondary school at age thirteen with the ambition to someday become an electrician. By this time I was an electrician of a sort, and I earned money on the side by repairing small appliances in Kampala. Although I was quite young, I nevertheless had burning with me an intense desire to keep on developing in my Islamic faith. Certainly I didn't understand Islam in all its fullness, but I was rooted deep in Muslim thought and culture. I loved everything about Islam. The Quran stood uncontested as my favorite book. To me, it was the revealed Word of God.

THREE
AMIN

On the morning of January 25, 1971, I arose as usual to
get ready for school. As was her normal practice, Mother
had been cooking in the kitchen long before I got up. Her
loving hands were kneading bread and preparing other
dishes that would be coordinated perfectly throughout the
day to care for the hungry members of her household.
My brothers and I enjoyed the delicious breakfast which
she had made, little realizing what news the day would
bring. While Hanif went off to primary school and
Mohammed and Hassen left for work, I simply walked
upstairs to begin school for the day. My secondary school
was located on the second floor of an old mosque, the
first floor of which served as our home.

The morning passed as usual and we were all dismissed
for lunch. I returned to school that afternoon only to be
startled by rumors that General Amin had taken over the
country. We were all sent home immediately upon the
arrival of our teacher, who, fearing a possible revolution,
was concerned for our safety.

"What are you doing home so early?" Mother asked with
a puzzled look as I entered the kitchen.

"Don't you know that Obote has been overthrown?" I

questioned. "General Amin's troops surrounded the parliament building last night and took it over."

My alarmed and frightened mother was not at ease until Mohammed came home and assured us that this was indeed good news. "Amin will take over Uganda and he is a Muslim!" he exclaimed. "We need to thank God for General Amin. Let's listen to Radio Uganda. Amin will be broadcasting all day."

His Excellency Al-Haji Field Marshall Dr. Idi Amin Dada, V.C., D.S.O., M.C., President for Life,[1] was clearly a liberator, according to Radio Uganda. The country had been discontented with Milton Obote, who had pushed taxes so high we were paying the government 60 percent of our meager income. He had also been about to force the women of Uganda—including Muslim women—to join the Army and to become laborers.

But now General Amin had saved us from Obote's oppression. The triumphant news echoed throughout all Uganda via the radio, television, and the newspapers. Political prisoners were released. Obote's secret police was disbanded. All day long, Amin was on the air promising new schools, roads, and hospitals for impoverished Uganda. The day was declared a holiday. Crowds danced in the streets and stomped on pictures of Obote. "Big Daddy" Amin was clearly the hero who had ousted the tyrant. But we considered the best news to be that Amin was a Muslim and we had even heard that he wanted to make Uganda an Islamic country. Over the radio he told us that the Muslim holy days would become public holidays for the entire country.

Who was this hulk of a man who appeared to be about 6' 4", weighing 280 pounds? Who was this self-proclaimed savior of Uganda who promised everything short of forgiveness of sins?

The son of an impoverished farmer of the Kakwa tribe, Amin dropped out of school at the end of the second grade (some say the fourth) and, at twenty-one, joined the King's

African Rifles as an assistant cook. For nine years he reigned
as the heavyweight boxing champion of the Ugandan
Army. He claims to have fought in Burma with the British
in World War II (though this is disputed) and in Kenya
against the Mau Mau Rebellion. He was given an officer's
commission in 1961, a year before Uganda received its
independence. Upon Obote's accession to power, Amin
became the armed forces chief of staff and the president's
right-hand man. Influenced by dreams and visions, Amin
said that back in 1952 he'd had a prophetic dream that
indicated he would some day lead the Army and then,
eventually, the country.

The merriment and flag-waving of January 1971 would
be short-lived. Amin's colorful buffoonery would soon turn
to sadistic paranoia. His personal physician said that he
was "not a personality to be underrated. True, he is nearly
illiterate; he is politically naive; he is violently unpredictable;
he is utterly ruthless. Yet he is also jovial and generous and
he has extraordinary talents—for practical short-term
action, for turning apparent weaknesses to his own
advantage, and for asserting his leadership among his gang
of thugs."[2]

Little by little the promises he made to the Ugandans
went up in smoke, first to be replaced by unpleasant
inconveniences, then by more severe demands. For
example, all British identification of roads, buildings, parks,
etc., would be changed to African names. Swahili was to
be the compulsory language—even for the thousands of
Asians, Americans, and Britons. Then we soon learned that
there would be little tax relief. Instead, the people of
Uganda had to finance a spending spree to expand and
reequip Amin's army. He promoted and overpromoted
soldiers and policemen on the spur of the moment.
Sergeants suddenly became heads of battalions. Tank
drivers became intelligence officers. And we learned that
an Army private had become the overall head of the
Intelligence Service through an instant appointment.

Many officers were forced to retire. Many more were slaughtered because Amin feared they still had leanings toward Obote. Amin handpicked all his personal assistants to safeguard his position.

The terrible eccentricities worsened as the weeks went by. Amin went crazy with power. Men had to bow before him. Women had to kneel. Obvious paranoia came to light when Amin announced that he felt Israel was plotting to poison the Nile River. At one time Israel and Uganda had experienced excellent relations. Amin had taken a paratrooper's course in Israel. Israel had supplied Uganda with some of its planes and weapons and had been asked to assist Uganda in building roads, houses, schools, and airports. But Amin suddenly ordered all Israelis out of the country and, as a consequence, millions of dollars worth of construction material lay idle and unpaid for.

His vehement anti-Semitism increased. As problems crept into his administration, he blamed his woes upon the Jews. He defended the Palestinian terrorist attack at Munich in 1972 and praised Adolf Hitler for his extermination campaign against the Jews. He declared that the Jews were not "working in the interest of the people of the world, and that is why [the Germans] burned the Israelis alive with gas in . . . Germany." "I'm going to be a second Hitler. I'll prove it to you," I heard him proclaim one day over national television. Eventually dual statues and busts would appear in Uganda—Idi Amin alongside Adolf Hitler.

Breaking all ties with Israel, he aligned himself instead with Libya's anti-Israel strongman, Muammer Quaddafi. After this Amin would nearly foam at the mouth with rage at the mere mention of Israel or of a Jew.

Inflation continued to skyrocket, tourism to Uganda declined, and the general state of the economy worsened. But to the Ugandans economic problems became secondary, for within two years Big Daddy began to bathe Uganda in blood. He was determined to rid the country of all opposition to his reign. The army would be purged of every member suspected of loyalty to former President Obote. His anti-Christian sentiment also became evident as a wave of persecution against the Christians began to grow.

The backbone of the Army came from two tribes—the Acholi and Langi, both of which had leanings toward Obote. The majority of these two tribes were professing Christians as a result of the tremendous missionary activity in Uganda over the last hundred years. This fact, coupled with his desire to rid the army of all disloyal elements, gave Amin a dual purpose in exterminating thousands of Acholi and Langi tribesmen and their families.

Radio Uganda was seldom turned off, but by now we didn't know what was fact or fiction if it came from Amin's office. Rumors were that Amin had his victims tortured before they were killed. His poorly trained soldiers were a law unto themselves. They raped and killed as they pleased, with hardly a reprimand from Amin. The soldiers became so bold with their newfound power and status that they openly assaulted Christians and political suspects right in the streets of Kampala. Word spread that Amin believed everyone was after his job, and for this reason he ruled by terror.

Soon Ugandan Christians and political suspects of any religion began to disappear. In some cases the victims had been overheard murmuring against Amin. More often they were not even guilty of that "crime," yet they became targets of Amin's "goon squad." Many times when soldiers picked up a victim in broad daylight, any onlooker who flinched, protested, or intervened became the next victim. All Uganda began to shudder as everyone anticipated a possible knock on his door late at night, and then a trip to jail, a torture chamber, or a grave in the Nile River.

During these days we sensed impending doom. Our earlier conceptions of Amin faded away. It was now obvious that he was thoroughly evil. But these dark days only served to draw our family closer together. We were always close—very close—but now our love and concern for each other deepened greatly. We valued each other more, we depended on each other more, and we cared for each other more. Our prayers were said with more intensity as we became more passionately devoted to Allah. God, we knew—and only God—could preserve us in these turbulent times.

FOUR
BLOOD BATH

Mother called me inside one hot afternoon. The tropical Ugandan climate was about to be interrupted by the usual afternoon thunderstorm. Without warning, the sky suddenly turned black, it thundered, the air was still for a while, then the wind blew, rain fell in sheets, and within minutes the sun peeked through the clouds again. But another kind of storm was brewing throughout the country as Amin's ominous presence was being felt in his own hideous way. My mother had summoned me inside to witness something of this on a special news bulletin over TV.

Though my mind was still occupied with my outside activities, she pointed to our small black-and-white television set. "This is why I want you close to home, Hassanain," she explained.

Suddenly my mind was staggered as I realized that a public execution was about to take place on live TV!

"The president has taken to showing his executions on television, Hassanain. We must pray even more that Allah will protect us. Our only hope is that we are devout Muslims. But we cannot even murmur against Amin! Do you understand, Hassanain? We cannot even murmur!"

I sat watching, frozen and speechless, as soldiers lined

up about a dozen prisoners against a wall. The prisoners' somber faces were then covered with black hoods. I wanted to turn away, yet couldn't. The shots rang out, and the bodies slumped—I could hardly believe what was happening before my eyes. It was a horrible scene—a grim reminder of the consequences of challenging Amin. Thoughts raced through my mind about our own fate, for soon there would be no restraint on the wholesale terrorizing.

We became constantly aware of danger, and every footstep behind us made us fearful that we might be attacked by one of Big Daddy's soldiers. People would disappear suddenly, and we all knew that disappearance usually meant death.

Idi Amin proved to be an outright tyrant, a vicious, savage despot of the worst kind. He established the State Research Bureau to carry out his barbaric acts of violence against the Ugandan people. The SRB was virtually a chamber of horrors for those unfortunate enough to find themselves within its walls. The guards would hammer men to death in about ten minutes. Women would have their throats slit. Some would die with the swift blow to the head with a twenty-pound sledge hammer. Other prisoners were forced to club each other to death. The lucky ones were simply shot. Many found themselves victimized by the sophisticated electronic equipment used by the 300 men and women employees involved in the sinister work.

Amin, however, was not restricted to the confines of the State Research Bureau. Many Ugandans were blown up in army barracks or jails, carved alive, or bound and tossed in the Nile River or Lake Victoria where they either drowned or were devoured by crocodiles. In fact, it has been reported that so many bodies were thrown into the Nile that divers had to retrieve some to clear the intake duct at the Owens Falls Hydroelectric Plant.

Big Daddy's agents were constantly in pursuit of dissidents. Often suspects would be stuffed into the trunks

of cars, never to be seen again. Anyone who offended a
soldier could be gunned down on the spot. Prisoners were
buried up to their necks in cesspools. Captives would be
shot in the knees, doused with gasoline, and set afire. The
inhabitants of entire villages were slain by machine gun
fire. Every civilian that could be found in Obote's home
town of Akoroko is said to have been slaughtered by an
unmerciful raid by Amin's marines. On the outskirts of
Masaka, one eyewitness reported seeing victims bound with
rope, flung to the ground, and shot. Their cries for mercy
were left ringing in the night air.

Every brutal killing was intended to consolidate Amin's
position as unassailable dictator. His reign of terror was
the epitome of barbarity. In his first year of power he
butchered an estimated 90,000 Ugandans. Before he was
deposed in 1979, the slain totalled about a half a million.

Not many nations have been able to claim a ruler who
practiced cannibalism. Uganda, unfortunately, is one of the
few holding that distinction. Its recent ruler was unabashed
about his taste for human flesh and blood. Neither did
he have any qualms about committing murder. He
personally shot the late archbishop Janani Luwum once
through the mouth and three times in the chest.[1]

A death dealer with an insatiable thirst for power, Amin is
described by Henry Kyemba, his former physician, as a
"thoroughly unbalancing and destructive force for Africa
and for the rest of the world. He will quarrel with anybody
in order to achieve any slight advantage. He never keeps
his word. He knows no morality. . . . He has proved himself
a liability to the Moslem cause, the Arab cause, the cause
of Africa, and above all, the cause of humanity."[2]

As people in other countries became aware of the blood
bath in Uganda, many shook a finger at Amin. Even a
prominent ambassador to the United Nations called him a
"racist murderer," yet for years no country took official
action against him. He turned almost exclusively to Arab
countries and to Russia for aid, arms, and supplies. Without

Arab aid in particular, Uganda's economy would have
collapsed.

Libya's President Quaddafi, obviously courting Amin to
the side of Arab extremists, said to the Ugandan: "You
are a prophet! Be brave and we will support you."[3] Later
Saudi Arabia's King Faisal visited Amin. He gave him
royal gifts—an enormous platter of solid gold and a gold
sword. Bishop Kivengere reports that King Faisal told
Amin, "With this sword, Muslimize your country." Certainly
not a sincere Muslim, Big Daddy was undoubtedly using
his supposed commitment to Islam as a pretense for
winning support and economic aid from the wealthy Arab
countries. It is claimed that had Amin remained in power
through 1979, he would have declared Uganda an Islamic
state, despite the fact that only ten percent of the population
is Muslim.

Perhaps the most misleading aspect of Amin is his
deceptively amicable character. He can be a congenial
entertainer one moment and a ruthless killer the next.
Many—both within Uganda and without—if not totally
deceived, have been sadly misled by Amin's mercurial
character. Many of his own countrymen liked his openness,
frankness, and clownish antics. His political unsophistication
appealed to the common people. But behind the alluring,
jovial nature lay a monumental oaf. A sampling of Big
Daddy's blundering rhetoric is sufficient to prove the point.

After suppressing an attempted coup, Amin, in an effort
to dissuade similar subversive activity in the future,
declared to the Ugandans: "If you are unhappy with me,
then kill me or make me resign and don't disturb the people
at night by running about shooting."[4]

At one point Big Daddy charged Britain with "planning
a 'land, sea, and air invasion' of Uganda. When it was
pointed out that landlocked Uganda is miles from any
ocean, Amin belittled British Foreign Secretary Sir Alec
Douglas-Home for betraying his 'ignorance about Africa'
by plotting a naval attack in the first place."[5]

Hardly one to withold his opinion, Amin, in addition to wishing former President Nixon a "speedy recovery from Watergate," had this to say to the Nobel Peace Prize nominee: "I should like to congratulate you for the nomination. However, I have reason to believe the organization that has nominated you merely wishes you to hear of the nomination so that you can recover from the Watergate affair. My reason for holding this view is that it is very discouraging for real peacemakers in the world to hear of your nomination . . . I am led to the conclusion that your nominators were not serious in their choice."[6]

Stanley Meisler, commenting on Big Daddy's diplomatic tactlessness, put it most aptly when he wrote: "There can be few more incredible communications in the history of diplomacy than his telegram to President Julius Nyerere of Tanzania . . . After denouncing Nyerere, Amin added, 'With these few words I want to assure you that I love you very much and if you had been a woman, I would have considered marrying you even though your head is full of grey hairs, but as you are a man that possibility does not arise.' "[7]

By no means should such bombast be taken too lightly. For with such outlandish statements Amin has demonstrated his gross instability and ignorance. And with such ignorance has come disgrace to Black Africa and the denigration of the human race.

Perhaps the greatest tragedy is the ignorance of those who continue to remain optimistic about modern man's ability to achieve world peace when, in the latter half of the twentieth century, such a demented and capricious despot has been allowed to rise and remain in power.

I have seen too much to believe, with the naiveté and delusion of the many today who somehow think that man's nature is basically good. I can only conclude that such reasoning stems from being boxed into a soft and affluent culture secluded from the larger world outside.

FIVE
BIG DADDY OR BIG DUMMY?

In August of 1972, Idi Amin announced his plan to
"Africanize" Uganda. Through his "Black is best" program
he insisted that Black rule for Uganda meant that the
thousands of Asians holding British passports must leave the
country. Big Daddy Amin claimed his decision to expel the
Asians came straight from Allah. "God was directing me to
act immediately to save the situation," he declared as
he vowed to make Uganda "the first genuinely Black
African state."

Until Uganda's independence in 1962, most Asians living
in the country held British passports, as this was the only
travel document available to these people living in what
was then a British colony. However, only 23,000 Asians
had taken out Ugandan citizenship since the country's
independence. The remaining 55,000 had just ninety days
to leave the country. Each "alien" family could take
out only $140 and twenty pounds of belongings per person.
The rest of its possessions—homes, furniture, automobiles,
and savings accounts—were to become the property of
Amin's government.

But where were the Asians to go? It was of no concern
to Amin. He just wanted us out. Our mother countries—

Pakistan and India—were overcrowded and underfed as it was. England didn't want the "colored immigrants." In fact, one English city, Leicester, went so far as to advertise in Kampala newspapers that Asians were to stay away because of crowded conditions. And adding to the nightmare was the fact that *no* other country seemed to want us.

Since my family and I were Ugandan citizens, it appeared that we would not be affected by the expulsion order. But the announcement soon came that the exodus was to include all Asians, regardless of civil status. Amin, however, due to pressure from other African governments, quickly modified the edict to include only those who could not prove Ugandan citizenship. Yet Amin would remain undaunted in his effort to get the Asians out. He had the citizenship papers reviewed, and, for whatever reasons, possibly two out of three Ugandan Asians lost their citizenship.

Amin's goon squads now took up a new crusade. Along with the purge of political and religious opponents they added an all-out attack on the country's 80,000 Asians. Drunken, moody soldiers barely able to handle a rifle began harassing and humiliating whatever Asian they wished. It no longer mattered that we were Muslims. Our one hope shattered, we found ourselves in the same camp as the rest: victims of Amin's erratic, menacing thugs.

It was very clear that Asians were not welcome in Uganda. There was deep resentment and hatred among many of the Blacks against the Asians—whether justifiable or not, I do not know. It is true that we ran most of the commercial and business interests within the country. However, few of the native Ugandans had the necessary business skills to do so. I do not believe that the Asians were exploiting the Africans to any significant degree, though I am well aware that such activity always exists among mixed ethnic and racial groups.

Amin's policy of Africanization proved to be one of his most blundering moves. It deprived Uganda of the very people who made the country's economy function. How was Amin, after such a sudden expulsion, to turn over the Asian industrial and professional affairs to the untrained Africans? Foreign analysts observed that at this point in Uganda's stage of development the Asians' expertise was essential. One observer correctly predicted in the fall of 1972 that within ten years Uganda would fall apart because of internal problems and pressures as a result of "kicking out its ablest citizens just as it most needs them."[1]

By August 1972 Big Daddy had driven Uganda to the brink of bankruptcy, primarily through excessive military spending. He therefore found a convenient scapegoat for the crisis in the Asians, who he claimed were "economic saboteurs," "milking the economy of the country." Some think, and probably rightly, that Amin's real reason for ousting the Asians was an attempt to divert attention from his own shortcomings as president. Another factor could well have been Amin's desire to gain a more widespread popularity among the various tribal factions. He undoubtedly hoped to alleviate much tribal strife and to bolster his own image by manipulating the traditional prejudices of the many black groups against the Asians.

It became apparent to my family and me that if we were to remain in Uganda, we would have little chance of staying alive. We therefore began to make plans to leave the country. My sister Zehra had married a Tanzanian several months before and had already moved to Tanzania with her husband. We thanked Allah for that. However, my brother Mohammed had also married at about the same time, so my sister-in-law Rahanna, who was now eight months pregnant, would have to flee with us.

Just as we were considering how to leave the country, Mohammed had to enter the hospital for dental surgery. From the day our father died we depended on him as the head of the family, but with the political unrest all around us we couldn't be sure if he was alive or not. We would make no plans until he came home from the hospital—if he came home at all.

Tension thickened as we heard gunfire around the clock. Fear-filled days ran into fear-filled nights. Soldiers seemed to be everywhere. We heard of friends being thrown from their homes. All Uganda was in a state of terror and we shuddered to think what the next day would bring.

Finally, Mohammed returned home safely from the hospital. He told us of Pakistanis and Indians—hundreds of them—coming into the hospital as victims of Amin's Russian-made rifles. Some of the patients had been riddled with bullets, yet many of them lived to walk to the hospital. We knew that only Allah could protect us from a similar fate. We trusted in him explicitly.

Our initial step to gain our freedom and safety began with the British Embassy. I was appointed to go to the embassy to hold a place in line while Mohammed acquired some application forms. We had no idea that the waiting would last three days and nights. Six hundred Asians were in line ahead of me, each as frantic and desperate as the other.

The fierce burning sun beat down upon us as the line inched forward a few steps every hour. We dared not talk among ourselves against Amin, for fear that some informer, planted in the line, might have us hauled away. Everyone kept his thoughts to himself while the time dragged on endlessly. The usual afternoon storm drenched us all and only nightfall brought relief from the blazing sun.

When there were but ten people between me and the doorway of the embassy, Mohammed came running to relieve me. He had just finished filling out the application forms. Exhausted and hungry, I was barely able to express my joy.

I trudged home wearily, wondering what would happen next. As I entered the house, mother greeted me with a loving embrace. I told her that all I wanted was something to eat and to go to bed. The three days and nights had taken their toll upon me.

Inside the embassy, Mohammed watched the staff scurry about the office. They seemed hopelessly overworked and as distraught with the situation as we were. But as yet they didn't have to fear for their lives. The British and the few Americans left in the country were subject to harassment, but not death.

Files and files of records had to be processed for each applicant. But at least now my brother was inside. He would have our papers signed, sealed, and on their way to England within an hour. So we thought.

When Mohammed's turn came, he stepped boldly to the window and faced a tired Englishman who looked at him with utter apathy through a wire screen. His voice seemed both mechanical and irritated. "Why should you go to Britain? What makes you think you belong there?"

"Because Britain ruled Uganda when my father was born here," Mohammed asserted confidently.

"You no longer have those rights. You'll have to move on."

"But we've been in line for three days, sir," protested Mohammed.

"Next," the Englishman announced looking beyond him.

Just like that! How could anyone have so little compassion?

The desperate man behind Mohammed pushed him out of the way. He too had left his family for three days and had no qualms about being overly intrusive.

When Mohammed finally made it home, he found us anxiously awaiting his report.

"Has England accepted us?" we asked enthusiastically.

"No," he sighed, "fifty thousand Asians are fleeing the country. It's all very complicated. It is easy for Amin to kick us out, but it's not easy for his people to fill out all the forms. England won't accept us. We'll have to try the

Canadian Embassy and trust God to send us wherever he wills. Hassanain, will you wait in line for us again while I fill out the forms?"

Disheartened, like the rest of the family, I replied drowsily, "Okay, I'll go first thing tomorrow morning."

About four hundred people were ahead of me in the Canadian line—four hundred tense, shoving Asians whose hour of doom was getting closer and closer. Amin would keep his word; there was no question about that. Any Asian not out of the country by the deadline would end up in a "transit camp"—just a step from the grave.

This time the line moved much more quickly. I felt fortunate that I had only twenty-four hours to wait before Mohammed relieved me. But the Canadian attendant seemed as unconcerned as the British one had been. Yet this time we got as far as giving the gentleman the statistics about our family.

"Canada will take you, your wife, and your brothers," the embassy spokesman informed Mohammed, "but not your mother or your grandmother. They're too old. You and your brothers can work in Canada, but the others cannot. The government would have to take care of them and I'm afraid it cannot do that. Would you like me to process you and the others?"

There was nothing to say. We would never leave our mother behind nor send her alone to another country. Muslims take care of their own and would never think of leaving a family member to the unknown.

That night we all sat around the radio hoping for at least a hint of direction as to what to do. Instead we only heard more threats and warnings to get out of the country. Cheerless and downhearted, we just sat there, wondering what would become of us. It seemed that all but Allah had abandoned us. But God, Mohammed assured us, would continue to see us safely through.

My brother's encouraging words would prove true sooner

than we thought. About 11:00 P.M., a special bulletin was aired over Radio Uganda: "The American Embassy has just announced that it will take two thousand Asians. They will begin interviewing applicants at 7:00 A.M. and then work around the clock until all two thousand Asians are fully processed."

Unspeakable joy began to swell in our hearts! A way of escape might be provided after all! We knew little of America, but judging by its television programs we were sure that the country was filled with violence. Rumors were that, since the United States was engaged in the Viet Nam War, any Asian sent to America would be drafted into the Army. But what did it matter? Our chances for survival would certainly be as good in Viet Nam or America as they were in Uganda.

"Hassanain, would you go down to the American Embassy now and wait in line?" requested Mohammed. "By morning there will be more than two thousand waiting to get in."

I left immediately. If I ran fast enough, I thought to myself, I might avoid a two or three-day wait in line, but if I was seen running by Amin's men, I would probably be shot on the spot. I decided to walk at a normal pace and to hope, with Allah's help, to be one of the first in the American Embassy waiting line.

A full moon shone brightly over my beloved Kampala as I walked toward the center of town. I was glad that the hour didn't reveal all that had happened throughout the city over the past several weeks. A gentle breeze blew against my face as I stepped lightly in the night air. I listened for any strange sound or sudden movement near me. The city was never quiet anymore, and a rustle in a nearby bush could spell danger. The twelve-block walk was the longest mile of my life.

The embassy building came into view at last—and only about one hundred persons were standing in line! We would make it after all, provided America wouldn't turn away the elderly. I hadn't felt such a surge of hope since the day Big Daddy came to power, promising us all an improved Uganda.

While the line was growing steadily to several hundred, nervous Asians waited through the night for the American Embassy to open its doors. I wasn't too surprised that there were relatively few people in line, knowing the rumors that were circulating about Asians being drafted into the Army if they went to America.

I thought it would take a day to process the one hundred ahead of me. But I was amazed at how fast the line moved along. It was obvious that the American staff was organized and efficient—something I hadn't seen in Uganda for months. They seemed almost as concerned about the desperate Asians as were the Asians themselves. It encouraged me to know that another country was concerned about helpless Asians whose few possessions would be confiscated by a foreign government.

Within only four hours Mohammed arrived as usual with the necessary forms. We submitted the applications and then headed home. We were told that it might be several days before we would hear from them, but the embassy official could see no reason why we wouldn't be allowed to go to America. I was sure that within a few weeks we would be out of Idi Amin's chaotic, hellish Uganda.

Nevertheless the days of waiting seemed like years. Except for Mohammed, we seldom left our home as we feared getting caught in the sporadic shooting we kept on hearing day and night. Mohammed continued to work a few hours a week, but it mattered little that he did, for we couldn't take the money with us.

On one occasion this extra work almost cost Mohammed his life. He was about to drive away from a curb when a soldier stepped in front of the company vehicle he was driving. Mohammed waved to the man to pass. But the soldier, misinterpreting my brother's motives, walked to the window and shouted, "Are you trying to tell me what to do? Who are you to be ordering me?"

"I wanted to let you pass," replied Mohammed.

Obviously looking for trouble, the uniformed man struck my brother in the jaw with the butt of his rifle. The car went out of control and crashed across the street.

The soldier ran up to Mohammed and asked, "Why did you crash?"

"I lost control when you hit me," Mohammed responded before he was struck with the rifle butt once again and made to lie on the sidewalk. The soldier then pressed the rifle muzzle to his head.

Another armed man came up and admonished the soldier, "Do you realize what you are doing?" At this the two men simply walked away. Had the other soldier not intervened, Mohammed could well have been shot.

When Mohammed came home that day and told the rest of the family what had happened, we all listened intently and with concern. Relieved that he wasn't harmed, my brothers and I couldn't help but laugh because we knew how stupid Amin's men were and such incidents were not uncommon. Even Mohammed had to laugh.

Uganda's economy was in shambles. With the country stripped of such a high percentage of its skilled businessmen and professionals the economy would soon come to a standstill. Under the new regime the coffee and cotton industries, the nation's two largest, slumped severely. In fact, the supply of sugar and coffee, which Uganda had previously exported, dwindled so low that the two commodities had to be imported. Factories had to be shut down for lack of parts or for repairs. Many shops continued to display impressive wares, but inside no merchandise was available. Amin was paving the way for his own doom. It would only be a matter of years before his foolish policies would determine his own fate.

So far, my family had experienced anxiety and fear but not actual separation. But an opportunity finally came to send our grandmother to Kenya. Since she was in her nineties, we thought that she could never endure the long trip to America. So we decided to leave her with her children in Kenya as she was a citizen of that country. And Uganda welcomed the loss of another elderly Asian.

SIX
FLIGHT FROM UGANDA

Three days after submitting the application forms we
received our liberation notice! The American Embassy had
approved our family's application! We made immediate
preparations to leave Uganda on East African Airways—the
Ugandan line. Idi Amin ordered all Asians to leave the
country on East African Airways only. He also doubled the
usual fare to the cities to which that line flew, and banned
all foreign airlines from landing in Uganda.

But the nightmare was far from over. Ahead of us were
days of inspections, searches, more intimidation, and the
final red tape required for leaving the country. To further
complicate matters, our departure from Uganda would be
during the month of Ramadan when all Muslims must fast
from sunrise to sunset. In addition to all the anxiety and
stress that we were undergoing at the time, this would
especially tax our strength.

The Fast is held during the ninth month of the lunar year
to commemorate the time when God revealed the Quran
to the prophet Mohammed. Muslims are forbidden to eat,
drink, or smoke throughout the day. We could take no
medication by mouth or by injection. While the Fast was in
effect, we could not even touch our mouths with our fingers.

We gathered all of our belongings together in one room and tried to decide what was most essential to take with us, for we were allowed to leave the country with only twenty pounds of luggage per person. Radio Uganda had announced that no valuables such as diamonds, gold, or jewelry could be taken out of the country. They were to become the property of the government. All of our money would also be confiscated by Amin—except for a mere $140.

As was the custom, Mohammed and Rahanna had received some gold jewelry when they were married earlier in the year. Now we had to decide whether or not we would try to keep it. Would it be better to start from scratch, penniless in America, or to risk the execution of our entire family? It was not an easy decision to make.

"Kishor mentioned that I could bring the gold to his family's shop and they could melt it down for us and make chains out of it," I suggested as we began to consider the matter.

"That sounds like a good idea," Mohammed responded.

"Well, Hassanain and Kishor have been friends for years, and if we can't trust Kishor, who can we trust?" added Mother.

As excruciating as it was to destroy our beautiful jewelry, the rest of the family agreed immediately. It was decided that we would try to bribe a guard. I took all of our gold jewelry to Kishor and his father who then melted it down and made three crude chains out of it. It was planned that after our inspection at the airport we would place the gold chains around our necks and wear them until we reached America, thus ensuring that we would never lose them.

The radio broadcasts were not mere threats. We heard of an Asian woman who was shot because she tried to leave the country with jewels hidden in her hair. She was gunned down in front of hundreds of other Asians as an example. An Asian surgeon had cut one of his arms open and embedded some diamonds under the skin. He then sewed himself up and covered his arm with a cast. The man made the fatal mistake of reaching down to pick up a briefcase with his "broken" arm. The security guards were quick to figure out his scheme and shot him on the spot.

Amin's men began to realize how clever the Asians were at concealing valuables. As a result their security grew tighter and their tempers shorter. The only hope of leaving Uganda with anything of worth was to bribe a guard. But if either the Asian or the guard were caught, both would be shot on sight.

Our devotion to our faith during these fear-filled days was binding us closer together than we had ever been before. Mohammed continued to have the strongest faith of us all. He assured us that despite our losses, Allah would provide everything we would need—and more besides—wherever he would send us.

By African standards our servants became wealthy after we gave them practically all we possessed. They were sad to see us leave, and we, in turn, were sad to be leaving them. But we were actually the most fortunate of Uganda's people; we were on our way to freedom, while the rest were condemned to remain in a fear-ridden, devastated country. We were not the real victims of Amin's madness, as were those left behind in his violent, bleeding Uganda. The coming years were to bring increasing chaos to a land already racked in horror.

We rode a bus to Entebbe Airport. Had we owned a car, we would not have driven it, for each automobile en route to the airport underwent an intense inspection every five miles. For us this would have meant five thorough searches. The chances of bribing five guards were impossible. Besides, we heard that some Asians never made it beyond all those checkpoints. Many of those who did were terribly humiliated. One woman was raped so many times on the way to Entebbe that she had to be hospitalized when her plane landed in nearby Kenya.

A few days from the deadline Amin said that the Asians could send out by air freight a few personal belongings after all. Some Asians eagerly packaged some of their special possessions and sent them to various checkpoints where they would be "guarded" until loaded onto the planes. While we were on our way to the airport we passed these checkpoint areas. All the boxes had been split open and the goods stolen by the soldiers and the police. We later found out that only a few packages ever left the country.

As our bus forged ahead toward Entebbe, we continued to thank Allah for assisting us in our escape to freedom. Before long, however, we faced a new problem. Aboard the outdated Ugandan bus as it jerked and shook its way along the twenty-five-mile road to the airport, Rahanna began to feel sick. She was in her last stages of pregnancy and we knew that under the circumstances any illness could be serious.

Finally the airport came into view. It was thoroughly congested. Our bus driver inched his way through the parking lot with the horn constantly blaring. Everyday from this place hundreds of Asians were leaving the only homeland they ever knew.

As we entered the terminal building I scanned the sea of frightened, bustling humanity. Hundreds of Asians were being searched meticulously, and were subject to the taunts of soldiers and police in the process. A handful of American airline personnel and a few British were also preparing to leave the country, but they didn't seem to have to undergo as rigorous a form of inspection as did the Asians.

We saw many friends at Entebbe and took the opportunity to exchange a few last words with them. It was a sad time. Hassen seemed especially grief stricken. I can remember him talking with some of his friends and crying with them because they didn't know if they would ever see each other again. Mother and I could not hold back our tears as we watched such a dismal scene. The time for

good-byes was almost over and all that remained was a
hopeful resignation to the situation.

Our first inspection line moved quickly. One at a time my
three brothers and I went behind a curtain where we were
stripped of our clothing and inspected by a guard. My
mother and sister-in-law were searched by another guard
behind a different curtain. We then proceeded to another
line to wait for the inspection of our suitcases.

Our three gold chains lay hidden in our luggage. We
knew all too well that if our bribe was not accepted we
would be slaughtered mercilessly. We had already seen an
Asian father dragged away from another line and taken out
of the terminal building. Just what he had done, nobody
seemed to know. His family looked on terrified but dared
not protest for fear of being arrested also. We heard gunfire
from outside the building, but there was no way of knowing
whether the man was being executed or if drunken soldiers
were merely shooting to amuse themselves. But, as was
usually the case, those who were dragged away were never
seen again. There were other such incidents. Confused
Asians wandered about the terminal waiting and hoping for
a family member to return. It was impossible to obtain any
information from the police or soldiers. Our closing hours
in Uganda were a fitting climax to nearly three months of
terror.

We prayed that the security guard would take the money
Mohammed was prepared to offer him. It seemed
unreasonable for an inspector to take the risk of accepting
any amount of money as a bribe, for he would be executed
immediately if he was suspected of anything less than blind,
unquestioning obedience to Amin. We kept praying
earnestly that Allah would see us safely through. If God
did not intervene, we didn't stand a chance.

Our turn in line finally came. We placed our luggage on
the counter for the security officer to inspect. As he began
to open the first suitcase, we just stood there, breathless
with suspense. Suddenly Mohammed flashed 400 shillings

(about $56) in front of him. Without hesitation, the
inspector quickly snatched the money and stuffed it in his
shirt pocket. He then merely glanced at the contents of
the suitcases and let us pass.

It was unbelievable! How we thanked God! Again we
had been spared by Allah's good favor. However, the
trauma of our ordeal was not over yet, for we had another
six or seven hours to wait before our flight would leave.
The atmosphere of the terminal was very somber and
sedate. The fleeing Asians said little as they feared giving
Amin's agents any grounds for their arrest. We waited and
waited, almost tasting our freedom, yet afraid that some last
complication might occur. Up to the last moment we feared
a possible bloodbath.

When our plane was ready for boarding, a line began to
move quickly but silently out of the congested terminal.
We had about fifty yards to walk before our feet would
touch Ugandan soil for the last time. It was a time of mixed
emotions. I was excited about what lay ahead, relieved
to be escaping the horror of Amin, but terribly saddened to
be leaving the land I truly loved. I was a bit nervous as
I found my way to a seat inside the airplane. This was to be
my first flight ever.

Moments later we soared off into the clear, blue African
sky. My eyes surveyed the beauty of the land below. While
I was enjoying my first panoramic view of Uganda, I was
perplexed at the same time at being fully aware that I might
never see my magnificent homeland again.

As the airliner headed for Rome, my home of sixteen
years eventually faded from sight. Italy would be the first
stop on our way to freedom. There more paper work and
red tape awaited us. Although the United States was our
ultimate destination, we knew little about the country. We
could only envision America as a land of violence. A
nightmare was over, but uncertainty clouded the future.

SEVEN
AMERICA

Rahanna's baby girl, Fizza, was born four days after our
arrival in Naples, Italy, about 350 miles from Rome. It
was during our month-long stay in a refugee camp outside
of Naples that we met with representatives of the Lutheran
Council in America. Through their Lutheran Immigration
and Refugee Service, they made all the arrangements
necessary for us to go to the United States.

When we arrived in New York City in late November of
1972, we were told that we could live in any of the fifty
states. We appreciated this very much, but we knew
virtually nothing about the various states or their climates.
We heard that California had warmer temperatures than the
chilly sixty degrees we felt in New York, but this was about
all we knew. Then some people from the Lutheran Welfare
Service in Minneapolis offered to sponsor our family in their
city. We had seldom experienced temperatures lower than
seventy degrees and nobody forewarned us of the arcticlike
winters of Minnesota. But it seemed as good a place as
any, so we accepted their invitation. We would catch an
early morning flight to Minneapolis the following morning.

New York City was an entirely different world from

anything my family and I had ever experienced. The New York skyline was shrouded in an unexplainable haze, and during our fifteen-minute cab ride to a hotel we saw nothing but a mass of steel and concrete, seemingly pointing into the clouds. Gone were the flowers and trees, and the smell of clean, pure air that we were so accustomed to.

"This city makes me think the world will soon come to an end," Mohammed remarked when we reached the hotel. We all knew that he was referring to the sexually lewd billboards and the tremendous number of liquor ads that we had seen as we passed through downtown New York. We had never seen such corruption and immorality.

None of us could absorb all the culture shocks—moving stairs, maid service, luxurious sunken bathtubs, and walls from which blasts of warm air came to heat our room—it was all very new to us. New York City moved at a hectic, chaotic pace. Everyone was in a hurry and no one had any patience. Yet we recognized that America was a land where everybody had the wonderful opportunity to do as they chose without government pressure. Although most people in New York appeared indifferent to those around them, the people from the Lutheran Welfare Service just couldn't do enough for us. We hoped they were typical of the people of Minneapolis.

There was so much to think about! That night I sprawled on a gigantic bed that I shared with two of my brothers. They talked into the night about many things, but I was deep in thought, knowing there would be a lot of adjustments to make in this new culture.

Minneapolis! Aboard a 747 we descended through the clouds toward the greenless land and houses below. Trees without leaves swayed in the autumn wind. Min-ne-ap—I couldn't even pronounce it. I thought it meant "many police" and I began to wonder what it would be like living in a city filled with police. In Uganda there was actually no difference between the police and the army and, due to the rumors circulating in Uganda, the thought crossed my mind that maybe we'd be sent to Viet Nam after all. Such were the fears of a misinformed refugee.

As we entered the airport terminal, we saw a group of people carrying placards and a huge banner. Their faces were full of anticipation as they began to walk toward us. We were really surprised when we read the large words on the banner: WELCOME TO MINNESOTA HIRJI-WALJI FAMILY! We couldn't believe it. Seeing all the smiling faces brought tears to my eyes. We never imagined that we'd get such a warm welcome.

At least two dozen people had come to greet us. They represented several Lutheran churches that were sponsoring our resettlement in America. These strangers went far out of their way in their effort to make sure the Hirji-Walji family felt accepted. "Who are these people?" I thought to myself. "Who are we that we should receive such attention?"

A pastor in the group approached me and asked, "Are you Hass-an-ain? Ah, did I say that right?"

"Yes, I am, and you pronounced my name pretty well," I replied.

"I'll take your suitcase and you can come with me. Some others will take care of the rest of your family. We'll meet them at your new home where we are going to have a reception for you," the pastor continued.

"A reception?" I questioned. "What's that?"

"Just a little gathering to make your family welcome in Minneapolis, Hassanain."

We walked for what seemed like blocks just to get out of the building. The enormous size of the airports in America astonished me. When I stepped outside, the reality of the frigid Minnesota climate blasted me in the face. I hadn't realized that such cold even existed. Why didn't they tell us we were being sent to the North Pole? This was no place for Ugandans who had baked in the hot African sun year after year. A piercing breeze caused me to literally shake from the cold.

"It's so *cold* out there!" I exclaimed, once the pastor and I got inside the car. My teeth were chattering so badly I could hardly talk.

"This is nothing, Hassanain," the pastor responded. "It's still mild out. It's going to get much colder yet. But you'll get used to it. We dress warmly here."

"Colder yet!" I blurted out, unaware that it was only twenty degrees above zero outside.

"Yep. Have you ever seen snow before?"

"No, sir, except on mountains and in refrigerators," I said jokingly.

The pastor was a pleasant fellow to talk with, and I felt he was truly interested in me. As we spoke with each other my mind was really occupied with the amazing things I was observing around me. He patiently answered all my questions and explained whatever puzzled me as we traveled along. I could not make any sense out of what he was telling me when he said that our destination was downtown Minneapolis. I wondered what "*down*town" could possibly mean. So much was totally different to me. The station wagon that I was riding in, like so many other things, was much larger than what I was used to. Also, the pastor appeared to be driving on the wrong side of the highway and I was sitting on the wrong side of the car. All the flashing traffic lights and the maze of arrows and signs only confused me. Buses and trucks of enormous size whizzed past us, convincing me further that America was a nation of speed—a country constantly on the move.

In about twenty minutes we drove up to a house near the downtown area of Minneapolis. As I walked up the front steps, I noticed that the rest of my family had already arrived. The house was full of people, some of whom I had already seen at the airport. In the middle of the dining room I saw a beautifully decorated table spread with a variety of delicious looking foods, but I doubted if my family and I could eat any of the meat, since a Muslim can eat only meat that has been slaughtered and prepared by another Muslim. Also, Muslims are not allowed to eat pork under any circumstances.

People welcomed us with outstretched hands of friendship. Their kindheartedness and goodwill were reflected in their happy and radiant faces. Such hospitality meant a great deal to us.

"This will be your home," the pastor told us toward the end of the evening. "All that is in it is yours."

We did not know what to say. The Lutheran Welfare Service and several Lutheran churches of Minneapolis had provided us with a new home, completely furnished!

After everyone left, we walked about the house, looking at all the gifts. We were really excited. It was a very, very joyful moment. The home contained a washer, dryer, refrigerator, and oven. The basement was stocked with a two-year supply of canned goods. There was a television set in the living room. Each bedroom had a radio. And to top it all off, the pastor had given us $250 in cash. We were overwhelmed. Our thoughts flashed back to what Mohammed had told us in Uganda: that God would provide everything we needed, and more besides. He reminded us that this had indeed come true.

As I reflect on the generosity of these good Christian people, I am very grateful for all they did for my family and me. I can especially appreciate the fact that, although they knew we were people of a different faith, they still genuinely accepted us. They were sincerely interested in us as fellow human beings. They freely gave and asked for nothing in return. We were humbled that Americans could be so benevolent to a homeless Asian family. How could one ever give thanks enough to a people who give you a chance to start over again?

My conceptions of America were beginning to change.

EIGHT
CAMPUS LIFE

When I came to America, I knew virtually nothing about Christianity. Yet, as is commonly conceived throughout much of the world, I thought of the United States as a "Christian" nation. Therefore, when I enrolled at Minneapolis Vocational High School to continue studying electronics, I was startled to find many of my fellow students basically nonreligious. They didn't seem to believe in much of anything. Some of them, quite frankly, seemed disillusioned about life in general.

Every year at the vocational school a day was set aside to expose the students to various cultural interests and exhibits. The occasion was called Human Relations Day. An opportunity was provided among the activities of the day for interested students to hear others tell about a particular religious faith or organization. Since I was the only Muslim in the school, I asked if I could speak to the students about Islam. I thought that many of them could be helped if they knew more about God and the Islamic way of life. Not only was I eager to share my faith with others, but I also looked forward to learning something about Christianity.

I spoke briefly on Human Relations Day, telling the students some basic facts about Mohammed and his teachings. Their response was encouraging. In addition to questions about Mohammed, I was asked what Muslims thought about Jesus. I told them that we believed Jesus was an important prophet who was never crucified and who did not die. He was taken into heaven and will return to earth someday and confess that he is not the Son of God.

Most of what the other students presented had to do with different church denominations. However, one student who spoke to us mentioned that a group of students at the school met for Bible study and prayer every Tuesday morning. Anyone who wanted to attend was welcome.

I was interested in learning more about Christianity, so I made it a point to accept the girl's invitation. Although much that I heard that day intrigued me, in no way did I question the truth of my own faith. In fact, I wanted to see these Christians become Muslims and I knew that I would have to have a good understanding of their faith if I was to persuade them that it was wrong. And how could I tell them I was right if I didn't know what they believed?

When I went to next Tuesday's meeting, I found out that the students were involved in Campus Life, a Christian outreach to high school students. Wendell Amstutz, the full-time director of the Campus Life Clubs in the area, shared his Bible with me as he led the group in a short discussion.

Though I understood little of what was said about the Bible, I was impressed with the lives of these students. They had warmth and compassion, understanding and love, not only for one another, but also for me. Their conduct and character stood out against that of the rest of the students. When I asked them just what the difference was, they told me they were Christians. This puzzled me, since I thought practically everyone in America was a Christian.

After the Campus Life meeting I began to ask several students throughout the school what religion they believed in. When they told me they were Christians, I was really confused. I simply could not understand how people with completely different outlooks on life could call themselves Christians. God was clearly foremost in the minds of the Campus Life students, yet many other students who regarded themselves as Christians appeared to live solely for their own pleasure, with hardly a thought about any kind of responsibility before God. Many of their lives reflected no concern for God whatsoever, but still—for some reason—they thought of themselves as Christians. I would learn much later of the distinction between Christians merely by *name* and Christians by *faith*.

I liked the Campus Life students. Their attitude about life was similar to mine. God was at the center of their lives and their chief concern was how to please him. However I believed they, as Christians, were not worshiping God as he ought to be worshiped. That first Campus Life meeting I attended I told Wendell Amstutz that I was a Muslim and asked him if I could speak to the group about Islam.

"Sure," Wendell replied enthusiastically. "Just let me know when you're ready. If you'd like, you can take over next Tuesday."

I was surprised that Wendell responded so favorably. His willingness to allow me to share my faith encouraged me. I hoped that some of the students would be interested in becoming Muslims.

The rest of the week I waited in anticipation of the upcoming Campus Life meeting. I was anxious to speak of Islam, while at the same time eager to get better acquainted with the Campus Life students. When Tuesday morning finally arrived, I spoke for about twenty minutes, sharing basically the same things I did on Human Relations Day. But I ran into a problem. I told the students that the Quran is the Muslims' holy book as is the Bible for Christians, but I did not have an English translation of the Quran to substantiate what I told them. The time went well, however, and some interest in the Muslim faith was created among the students.

For the rest of the year, I continued going to the Tuesday morning Bible study and made many friends with the Campus Life students. Although I was a Muslim, they enjoyed my friendship, and I enjoyed theirs. These students were steadfast in their faith and I knew it would be difficult to persuade them to become Muslims. Nevertheless, my desire to become an effective witness for my Islamic faith remained.

Although I was interested in what Christians believe, I did not want to buy a Bible at this time. I saw no need for it. I considered it a waste of time to seek for truth in anything other than the Quran. What I needed to know about Christianity I would learn from the Christians themselves, for I regarded the Bible as the devil's book—a corrupted version of a collection of revealed books which God "sent down" to the prophets Moses, David, and Jesus. I was afraid that if I bought a Bible God would in some way punish me for it.

Actually, for me to have been antagonistic towards the Bible was contrary to the teachings of my own Scriptures, for the Quran clearly testifies to the authenticity of the Bible. In support of the Old Testament the Quran states the following:

Indeed, We[1] gave the Children of Israel
the Book, the Judgment, and the Prophethood,
and We provided them with good things,
and We preferred them above all beings.
We gave them clear signs of the Command: [Surah
    (chapter) 45:15, 16a/16, 17a].
Surely We sent down the Torah [the five books of Moses
    or the Old Testament in general], wherein is
guidance and light; thereby the Prophets
who had surrendered themselves gave judgment
for those of Jewry, as did the masters
and the rabbis, following such portion
of God's Book as they were given to keep

and were witnesses to. So fear not men,
but fear you Me; and sell not My signs
for a little price. Whoso judges not
according to what God has sent down—
   they are the unbelievers. [Surah 5:48/44]

Not only does the Quran speak favorably of the New
Testament, it claims to confirm it:

And We sent, following
in their footsteps, Jesus
son of Mary, confirming
the Torah before him;
and We gave to him
the Gospel [or New Testament in general], wherein
is guidance and light,
and confirming the Torah
before it, as a guidance
and an admonition
unto the godfearing.
So let the People of the Gospel judge
according to what God has sent down
therein. Whosoever judges not
according to what God has sent down—
   they are the ungodly.
And We have sent down to thee the Book [Quran]
with the truth, confirming the Book [Bible]
that was before it, and assuring it [or *and a protector
   over it*].
   [Surah 5:50-52/46-48]

Since "there is no suggestion in the Quran that the
Gospel given to Jesus was different from the canonical
Gospels held by Christians"[2] the obvious contradictions
between the teachings of the Bible and those of the Quran
means that only one of the books can truly be a revelation
from God. In fact the Quran, in stating that its message

confirms, and is in harmony with, the Judeo-Christian
Scriptures, shows itself to be clearly false—at least
concerning what it has to say about the Bible. To avoid
this dilemma, Muslims claim that the Scriptures revealed
prior to the Quran have been largely lost. The Bible we
have today, claim Muslims, does not consist of the original,
"uncorrupted" books sent from God.[3]

To support this view they appeal to the following passage
from the Quran:

> And there is a sect of them twist their tongues
> with the Book, that you may suppose it part of
> the Book, yet it is not part of the Book; and they
> say, "It is from God," yet it is not from God,
> and they speak falsehood against God,
>   and that wittingly. [Surah 3:72/78]

It is important to note that the Quran—which is the
supreme authority for Muslims—does not say that the *text*
itself was tampered with. It merely says that a group of
people distorted the Scriptures with their *tongues*.[4]

The Quran, in urging men to believe and obey the
Bible, is being inconsistent, for the Bible repeatedly affirms
that Jesus Christ is Lord over all—a message Mohammed
emphatically denied. Declares the Quran:

> Say you: 'We *believe* in God, and
> in that which has been sent down on us . . .
> and that which was given to Moses and Jesus
> and the Prophets, of their Lord; we
> make no division between any of them, and
> to Him we surrender.' [Surah 2:130/136]
> Say: 'People of the Book, you do not stand
> on anything, until you *perform*
> the Torah and the Gospel, and what was sent
> down to you from your Lord.' [Surah 5:72/68]

As Mohammed is supposed to have been illiterate, he undoubtedly never knew what the Bible really taught. Any contact he did have with Christianity was probably with heretical sects known to have been in his vicinity during his lifetime.

Unfortunately, many Muslims are raised to look down upon and to disdain Christianity, even though they know little about the religion. Few Muslims have even a slight interest to learn anything about the Christian faith, or the Christian Scriptures. Yet, even Mohammed was admonished by God to inquire of Jews and Christians about any doubts he might have concerning his own revelations. Surah 10:94 says:

So, if thou [Mohammed] art in doubt regarding
what We have sent down to thee, ask
those who recite the Book before thee.

Both Muslims and Christians are exhorted in their Scriptures to have a friendly attitude toward one another.[5] The Quran honors Christians in that it says "the nearest of them in love to the believers [Muslims] are those who say 'We are Christians' " (Surah 5:85/82). Christians and Muslims must not argue, and they must deal kindly with each other. Perhaps this is the most important thing for each to remember in their relations with one another. The Quran states this clearly in Surah 29:45/46:

Dispute not with the People of the Book
save in the fairer manner [or *unless in kindly sort*]
    except for
those of them that do wrong; and say,
"We believe in what has been sent down
to us, and what has been sent down to you;
our God and your God is One, and to Him
    we have surrendered."

The Bible says the following to Christians:

And the Lord's servant must not quarrel; instead, he must be kind to everyone, able to teach, not resentful. Those who oppose him he must gently instruct, in the hope that God will grant them repentance leading them to a knowledge of the truth, and that they will come to their senses and escape from the trap of the devil, who has taken them captive to do his will. [2 Tim. 2:24-26]

NINE
SCREAM IN THE DARK

During the summer of 1973, members of a nearby
Lutheran church invited me to attend a Billy Graham
Crusade at the Minnesota State Fairgrounds. I consented to
go because I had heard that Billy Graham was very
influential in leading people to Christ. I thought that I could
learn much about Christianity from this man that would
enable me to more effectively win my Christian friends to
Islam.

I sat in the front row of the grandstand as I listened
intently to Dr. Graham speak. His message of salvation and
forgiveness of sins through Christ alone disturbed me
greatly. I was angered to see such a large crowd exposed
to this forceful and convincing presentation of what to me
was a false religion. When the invitation was given to
receive Christ, hundreds of people made their way toward
the platform in front of the grandstand. I was moved with
jealousy because I wished that I could bring as many to
Islam.

Furious, I got up from my chair and pushed my way
through the crowd. Because of the large number of people
who had made their way forward, I could not get to the
platform. When I got as close as I could, I pointed my finger

at Billy Graham and shouted, "You are the first person who will go to hell for teaching the wrong religion!"[1] Mr. Graham's head remained bowed and his eyes closed.

I walked away infuriated and waited in the parking lot for the rest of our group. Despite any Quranic admonitions to the contrary, I hated Billy Graham because he was so successful in his ministry.

That fall I again returned to Minneapolis Vocational High School. Campus Life was preparing for its big fall event, "Scream in the Dark." Each year as a fund-raising project the students involved in Campus Life took an old abandoned house and turned it into a "haunted" house. Each night for a week hundreds of teenagers would come for an evening full of Halloween thrills and chills.

Wendell Amstutz asked me if I'd like to be a "monster" in the haunted house. I thought it was strange for Christians to dress themselves up to look like monsters, but it sounded interesting and I decided to give it a try. After all, it would be my first experience of Halloween.

We all arrived early Monday evening to make the final preparations for the first night of adventure for the week. The costume and mask I was given made me a hideous sight. What would these Campus Life people think of next? We were told to find some inconspicuous place from which to leap out and scare anyone passing by.

At one point in the evening before the teenagers began to arrive, I was wandering about the house when someone switched off the lights. It was pitch black. I soon heard soft steps coming toward me. For lack of anything else to do, I just stood there, listening as the steps drew closer and closer, until all of a sudden someone collided with me.

"Oh, I'm sorry!" came a girl's voice as the lights came on again. "Are you okay?"

It was another "monster" that looked so terrible I couldn't help but shriek. Then I laughed. *Here I am, a monster,* I thought to myself, *scared by another monster!* "I'm fine, thank you," I told her.

"Boy, you scared me," she exclaimed. "By the way . . . we haven't met, have we? My name is Carol. What's your name?"

"Hassanain."

"What was that again?" she asked, puzzled.

"Oh, that's Has-san-ain," I repeated, realizing that my name was strange to her as were many American names to me.

"What kind of name is that?"

"It's a Muslim name. It has to do with my religion."

We could hear the voices of several other young people heading our way, so we decided we had better find our positions for the night. As we parted, each of us took notice of where the other was headed.

"Maybe we'll see each other again," said Carol.

"Yeah, maybe. It was nice meeting you."

The next day I rode my bike to school as usual. I left an hour early to make it to our regular Tuesday morning Campus Life meeting. A few blocks from the school someone threw a rock and hit me in the head. I lost my balance and coasted into a parked car. My body slammed into the vehicle with a thud and then I felt a burst of pain as my head hit the ground. Everything became fuzzy. The next thing I knew I was walking into the Campus Life meeting with everyone staring at me.

Then I realized why they looked so shocked; I was scraped up and bleeding. I could vaguely remember the accident, but that was all. They all insisted that I go to the nurse's office and one of the kids took me there. The nurse thought I should see a doctor, but I told them I was fine. However, they gave me an ice pack for my head and said that I should go home. As one of the nurses rolled me in a wheelchair out of the building I was startled to see a huge crowd of students gathered outside. One of them asked me excitedly, "What happened? What happened?" Before I had a chance to answer, the nurse assured him that everything was all right. While I was being driven home,

I asked the nurse why all the students were outside and seemed so troubled when they saw me. I found out that the school was in the midst of a fire drill and upon seeing me they must have thought that there really was a fire!

My mother's face went pale as she saw me with an ice pack on my head, being led up the front steps by a nurse. She quickly ran out to help me into the house.

"Are you okay?" she questioned as Rahanna came running up.

The nurse explained the situation, and left with all of us giving her our thanks and appreciation. I walked into my room and lay down on my bed. Concerned about my condition, my mother and Rahanna persuaded me not to go to the haunted house that night.

Wednesday afternoon I was home for about ten minutes before the phone rang and Mother answered it. In our Muslim culture we never dated or sought to establish any kind of relationship with a member of the opposite sex before we were married. Therefore, when my mother heard a girl's voice on the other end of the line, she said to me with a strange look on her face, "Hassanain, the phone is for you."

Wondering who it might be, I took the receiver. "Hello," I said curiously.

"Oh, hi, Hassanain, I'm Carol," came a meek voice. "We met in the haunted house the other night, remember? I heard you were in an accident and I've been worried about you. How are you feeling now?"

Surprised, I simply said, "I'm fine, thank you." Perplexed by her apparent concern for me and irritated that I had received a phone call from a girl, I continued, "You don't even know me—what do you care? Why are you so troubled? I'm the one who got into the accident, not you."

"Well, Hassanain, that's what friends are for," Carol responded kindly.

I sensed something about her that I have seen in very few people. She had a genuine heart of compassion. However, not at all enthusiastic about her phone call, I replied rather sharply, "I just don't know what to say now. I've got to go. Good-bye."

My thoughts raced back to Monday night before I met Carol when I had asked Allah to provide some friends for me. But, because of our customs, I was not interested in having a girl for a friend. The "Scream in the Dark" week did bring many friends though, most of whom were active in Campus Life.

TEN
THE LIVING END

That fall I kept on going to the Campus Life meetings mainly because I had become good friends with several of the Christians within the group. Actually, these Campus Life students were about the only people I had any interest in getting to know. My ideas and values clashed much too sharply with the libertine attitudes and life-styles of most of the other students. And I was as determined as ever to see some of these Christian students become Muslims.

I began to learn quite a lot about the Christian faith and was eager to continue learning more. Much of what I had come to know about the Bible prompted me to more closely examine my own faith and to ask the students an endless stream of questions about Christianity.

I continued to have difficulty understanding the differences between all the people who called themselves Christians. I was told that not everyone who called himself a Christian really was. Before anybody could rightly consider himself a Christian, he had to be "born again," a term which made little sense to me at the time. I found this teaching rather strange, since all one has to do to become a Muslim is to recit the standard Islamic confession affirming that there is only one God and that Mohammed

is his prophet. A person is either a believer in God and his
prophet Mohammed or he is an unbeliever.

But to be a Christian it is necessary for one to be actually
transformed by the power of God. This comes about when
a person turns his life over to God by taking Christ as his
own Savior. When somebody acts in faith, in *receiving*
Christ, God, in turn, acts in *giving* new life to that individual.
As the person is given new life, he is born again, spiritually.
But one need only change his intellectual beliefs to become
a Muslim.[1] He must, of course, thereafter live a life in
conformity to Islamic law, but he does so by his own
capabilities, not by a changed life empowered by the Spirit
of God.

My view of many of the central themes of Christian belief
was typical of the misunderstandings that prevail
throughout the Muslim world. I was especially puzzled by
the concept of Jesus as the "Son of God." Since I
considered Jesus to be a great prophet, many Christians
would ask me if I also believed that he was the Son of
God. I thought, as do virtually all Muslims, that when
Christians speak of Christ as the Son of God they mean
that Jesus was the physical child of God and Mary. Since I
did not believe that God has children the way people do,
I did not believe that Jesus could be both a prophet and a
son of God. However, I did believe that God caused Mary
to conceive while a virgin by his own miraculous
intervention, for the Quran states this explicitly in Surah
3:47. I thought that Jesus, having been born of the virgin
Mary, could properly be called the son of Mary, but not
the son of God. But I was seriously mistaken in my view of
the biblical teaching of Christ's Sonship.

I understood the title, "Son of God," not in the spiritual
sense of Christ's eternal relationship with the Father,
but in a physical sense. To me, God's having a son by Mary
implied that he and Mary were husband and wife. Like
most Muslims, I confused this with the doctrine of the
Trinity. I took the Trinity to consist of Father (God), Mother

(Mary), and Son (Jesus), all of whom Christians worship
as three gods. Little did I realize at the time that these
erroneous views are as repulsive to Christians as they are to
Muslims.

Mohammed himself misconstrued the biblical teaching at
this point. The pagan Arabs of his time worshiped particular
idols called the "daughters of God." As "pagan deities
were male and female and had children,"[2] perhaps he
took the biblical term, "Son of God," in an analogous way
to this early Arabian usage. Also, there is evidence to
suppose that Mohammed was influenced in his
understanding of biblical doctrine by certain heretical
Christian sects known to have been active in Arabia during
his lifetime. The extreme veneration given to Mary by some
of these "Christians" undoubtedly affected his views.[3] It
can be seen from the following passagaes of the Quran
how easy it is for Muslims to misapprehend such crucial
Christian doctrines as the Trinity and the eternal Sonship
of Christ:

People of the Book, go not beyond the bounds
in your religion, and say not as to God
but the truth. The Messiah, Jesus son of Mary,
was only the Messenger of God, and His Word
that He committed to Mary, and a Spirit from
Him. So believe in God and His Messengers,
and say not, "Three." Refrain; better is it
for you. God is only One God. Glory be
to Him—that He should have a son! [Surah 4:169/171]
    And when God said,
    "O Jesus son of Mary,
    didst thou say unto men,
    'Take me and my mother
    as gods, apart from God'?"
    He said, "To Thee be
    glory! It is not mine to
    say what I have no right to. [Surah 5:115/116]

In this regard I could not conceive of why Christians would refer to God as their "heavenly Father." The thought of addressing God as "Father" was entirely foreign to me. Neither did I have any idea of what the Bible meant when it spoke of Christ as the only begotten Son of God. The Holy Spirit was also an enigma to me. To the Muslim mind a spirit is a created being, whether it be a man, an angel, or a demon. I did not think of the Holy Spirit as God, but as that glorious angel whom God used to reveal the Quran to Mohammed.

Because I was so inquisitive, some of the Christians at the school, both involved in Campus Life and not, suspected that I was interested in becoming a Christian. So anxious were they to bring me to Christ that they began to force their beliefs upon me, and I resented this. Their constant attempts to get me to accept Christ were not only futile, but they aggravated me greatly.

Although their motives were undoubtedly good, they did not realize that my interest in Christianity was solely that I might use whatever knowledge I gained to enable me to some day persuade them to become Muslims. I was not open to considering Christ. He was not an option for me because I was fully convinced of the truth of Islam. Sadly, they completely failed to understand the nature of my wholehearted Muslim faith. Their pressure tactics really led me away from Christ. It wasn't what they said that bothered me so much, it was the way they approached me. Their insistent and irksome ways brought me to the point where I didn't want to listen anymore. I even suspected that some sought to make friends with me, not because they were interested in me as a person, but because of the ulterior motive of winning me to their faith. Had I been exposed only to these particular Christians, I would never have been attracted to Christianity.

Nevertheless, on the whole I very much liked the Christians at Minneapolis Vocational High School and I found the Campus Life activities to be both interesting and challenging. Although Carol did not attend the vocational school, I had come to know her during the "Scream in the Dark" week and through other Campus Life activities involving students from various high schools. She, especially, stood out to me as an exceptionally fine person. There was just something about Carol which appealed to me. She knew how intensely committed I was to Islam, yet she befriended me as I was without attempting in any way to convert me. For some reason she never shared her faith with me, yet I knew she was a deeply devoted Christian, perhaps more so than the others I knew. Her life reflected well the truth of the song which I heard the students sing so often: "They'll know we are Christians by our love."

The most significant influence in my life at this time was a large conference I attended in December called "The Living End." Sponsored annually by Youth for Christ and Campus Life, this event provided an opportunity for high school students throughout the area to gather together at the end of the year for an extended weekend of Christian fellowship and training. Through various workshops, seminars, and lectures, all the participants received instruction and encouragement in several aspects of the Christian life. I went to the conference, despite its Christian orientation, because I felt like getting a change from the routine of things and enjoying a weekend away with my Campus Life friends.

The conference proved to be a very stimulating experience. It seemed that the more knowledge I came to acquire, the more questions I began to ask. I was forever trying to make sense out of this Christian religion. Most Muslims simply ignore Christianity and make no attempt to gain even a basic understanding of it. Many have an obvious smugness about them regarding Islam and are content to leave Christianity well enough alone. Generally, Muslims are held captive by the very cultures in which they live, in that they are restrained by social pressure and denied the right to question their own religion or to investigate another. If I had not come to America I might never have given Christianity a second thought. However, I felt that, since several of my friends were Christians, it was fitting that I should try to understand their faith. These friends were so sincere in their beliefs that I had a genuine concern for them that they might direct their attention along what was to me the true path—Islam.

I was perplexed at the response I would get from some of the students when I asked them about their faith. When I raised an objection they had not previously heard or asked them for clarification, they would often not have an answer for me.

"But you must believe it, anyway," they would object, seemingly for lack of anything else to say. "If you will just accept Christ first, then the Holy Spirit will make it clear to you."

"That makes no sense at all," I would argue. "How can I know you are right unless I understand what you are saying? You can't expect me to believe what you say if I can't understand it, can you? In Islam it's different. No one is expected to become a Muslim until he first understands the faith. Then he accepts it."[4]

Nonetheless, my questions did not cease and several of the unfamiliar Christian teachings were becoming clearer to me throughout the course of the conference. I was beginning to see that Christianity is in a class all by itself. In all the other religions of the world, man must strive to reach for God, whereas the Bible teaches that it is God who reaches for man. It is as if God were stretching forth his hands beckoning an unresponsive and lost humanity, "Come to me . . . and I will give you rest" (Matt. 11:28). In the final analysis, it is not man who seeks God, but God who seeks man. Nor is it what man does for God, but what God does for man. God takes the initiative and yearns to show his love for man. Mankind is loved by God unconditionally. In Islam, however, man must himself work to win God's favor, for God's love is conditional—that is to say, God will love someone *if* that person loves him, does what is good, or repents.[5] No matter what one may do for Allah, he can never be sure that Allah will accept his efforts.

I had no concept of any kind of relationship with God. God was distant. He was master, I was slave. There was no real intimacy. Mine was the ultimate in what is generally thought of as religion: myriads of religious laws and duties that must continually be performed to prove one's love for God. As a Muslim, I had everything mapped out for me as to what God required of me. It was a cold legalism compared to the Christian faith.

Seen in this light, Christianity is, in essence, a *relationship,* not a *religion.* One's religious life is not structured into a formal system like that of Islam. The stress is on intimate fellowship between God and man, not the performance of religious duties. As a Muslim I recited prescribed prayers to God in Arabic, while the Christians prayed spontaneously out of their hearts and in their native language.

Above all, it became increasingly apparent to me that my Christian friends really did have a sense of having been forgiven by God. They actually claimed to have the complete assurance of their forgiveness and acceptance by him. It was no wonder that they seemed so joyful most of the time. When I saw the inner joy and confidence that they experienced, I knew that there was more to their Christian faith than I had supposed. I was told that when one turns to Christ, God forgives all his sins: past, present, and future. This I found especially baffling. I could not comprehend how or why God would forgive a person's sins which he had not yet committed. I never knew whether my sins were forgiven even though I was careful to observe all that was demanded of me in the Quran and Islamic tradition. I would never know until the dreadful day of judgment how I would fare in God's sight. My righteous deeds would be weighed against the bad and my eternal destiny would be left hanging in the balance. If the balance fell in my favor, I would go to heaven; if not, to hell. Islam offers no assurance in this life.

I was discovering, however, that the Bible resounds with a message of a completely different order. The glorious thing about Christianity is that one's assurance of salvation does not rest on any works of man, but upon specific promises of God. If one does what God says to do, God will do as he promised. There are no strings attached. It is on this basis that the Apostle John could say, "I write these things to you who believe in the name of the Son of God so that you may know that you have eternal life. This is the assurance we have in approaching God: that if we ask anything according to his will, he hears us" (1 John 5:13, 14).

The Bible states that God has done everything necessary for man's salvation. All one needs to do is to accept—to act upon—what God has already done. God offers salvation to any who will take it and one has only to receive it like a gift. "For it is by grace you have been saved, through faith—and this not from yourselves, it is the gift of God—not by works, so that no one can boast" (Eph. 2:8, 9). As a Muslim, I had to work hard to try to gain salvation. The Christian faith is entirely opposed to a system of works. God requires only faith—complete trust and confidence in the saving merits of the Lord Jesus Christ. By faith one appropriates to himself what Christ has already done for him. Salvation is free! Islam has nothing to compare with this.

Previously I had spurned Christianity as an easy religion. I thought Christians were lazy. I accused them of not being able to fast for a month as I did during Ramadan. There appeared to be no laws for Christians to keep or duties to perform. It seemed foolish to me. But yet, the pieces of the Christian puzzle were coming together and my perspective was beginning to change. I started to wonder which religion might really be more in keeping with the character of God.

Doubts about Islam begin to prick away at my mind, and this frightened me. To question my faith was a grave sin. It was tantamount to heresy. I did not dare to imagine that Christianity may be true. To do so would incur the wrath of God. I feared divine punishment, yet I could not escape the logic of my own mind. I felt a storm rising within me.

One evening midway through the conference I plopped myself on a couch in dismay. It seemed as though a cloud was hanging over me. I was terrible depressed. Churning within me was the confusion of many thoughts—the Christian teachings of the Trinity, the Son of God, the assurance of the forgiveness of sins, God as the heavenly Father, Christ being crucified, buried, and raised to life again—all this called to question years of entrenched Islamic convictions. I was having to fight to retain my faith.

Christianity and Islam were at odds with each other and I was feeling the struggle within my own soul. I realized that not everything is as clear-cut as Muslims are led to believe. The biblical account of Christ reveals a far different picture from that presented in the Quran. The prophet *Isa* (Arabic for Jesus), though highly honored in the Quran, could not match the One who "was declared with power to be the Son of God by his resurrection from the dead: Jesus Christ our Lord" (Rom. 1:4). No prophet of Islam had ever been raised from the dead.

The purpose of several of the Quran's references to Jesus is to explain away what the Bible emphatically asserts about him as true. The entire New Testament repeatedly proclaims that his primary mission on earth was to die a sacrificial death on our behalf, while the Quran categorically denies this. On the one hand the Bible affirms the following, where Jesus says,

The reason my Father loves me is that I lay down my life—only to take it up again. No one takes it from me, but I lay it down of my own accord. I have authority to lay it down and I have authority to take it up again. This command I received from my Father [John 10:17, 18];

and where the angels at the empty tomb say,

Why do you look for the living among the dead? He is not here; he has risen! Remember how he told you, while he was still with you in Galilee: "The Son of Man must be delivered into the hands of sinful men, be crucified and on the third day be raised again." [Luke 24:5-7]

On the other hand, the Quran says this:

And for their unbelief, and their uttering
against Mary a mighty calumny,
and for their saying, "We slew the Messiah,
Jesus son of Mary, the Messenger of God"—
yet they did not slay him, neither crucified him,
only a likeness of that was shown to them.
Those who are at variance concerning him surely
are in doubt regarding him; they have no knowledge
of him, except the following of surmise;
and they slew him not of a certainty—
no indeed; God raised him up to Him; God is
    All-mighty, All-wise. [Surah 4:155, 156/156-158]

What to the Bible is the focal point of its message, is to the Quran a matter of mere conjecture. It is inconceivable to the Muslim mind that God would allow any of his prophets to suffer humiliation and shame at the hands of their enemies. For Jesus to have been crucified would have meant complete failure and defeat—something God would never have allowed. I thought that God had miraculously delivered the prophet Isa from his captors, taken him alive into heaven, and substituted someone else in his place who was then crucified. Since the Quran maintains that Jesus will experience death, I believed, like the majority of Muslims, that he will come back to earth, testify to the truth of Islam, and later die.

But what to the Muslim is unthinkable, to the Christian is the glory of his faith. Not only does the Bible contradict what Muslims believe about the death of Christ, its main emphasis is on the recurring theme of sacrificial, substitutionary atonement—in the Old Testament, in the sacrificial system instituted by God through Moses, and, in the New Testament, in the sacrifice of "the Lamb of God, who takes away the sin of the world" (John 1:29). Islam, in denying the crucifixion of Jesus, is repudiating the very essence of the message of the *Injil* (New Testament) which the Quran claims to confirm. Surely if the *Injil* has been corrupted as Muslims suggest, its predominant theme would have remained intact. If not, the *Injil* Mohammed avowed to confirm is unknown to history. It would have to be an entirely different book than the New Testament which Christians have been using since five hundred years before Mohammed's time.

The problems with which I wrestled as I sat on the couch that dismal evening were ones which I had to force myself not to consider. It was excruciating. I had come to know facts which were not easily evaded. All the prophets, including Mohammed, were sent to point the way to God, but now I was confronted by Jesus, who came pointing to himself and saying, "I am the way and the truth and the life" (John 14:6). If I were to turn my life over to Christ as God in the Bible summoned me to do, it would lead to a bitter conflict with my family—something I dreaded to think about. My family was more precious to me than anything else on earth. To be ostracized from its life was practically the same as being rejected by God. The thought was incomprehensible! I could never permit it to happen. My family, the Quran, Jesus, Islam—it was all tormenting me. My head was bowed in frustration.

Then along came Carol. I had seen her before at the conference, but had not spent much time with her.

"I haven't seen you around much, Hassanain. I didn't even see you at dinner," she said, with a curious look on her face.

"I know, I didn't feel like eating today. I haven't been feeling very well," I said sluggishly.

"Is there anything I can do for you?"

"No. There is nothing you can do for me. There is nothing anyone can do for me, except myself," I replied rather harshly.

"Hassanain, I can't leave you here sitting around doing nothing," Carol remarked with that soft, caring voice of hers.

"I'll be just fine," I retorted, somewhat irritated. "Just leave me alone."

Carol went away looking sad. I knew she could tell something was wrong. My despondency must have been written across my face. She was a sensitive, kind person and I felt bad that I had responded to her as coldheartedly as I had. But the turmoil that was boiling within me—my family, Islam, Christ—it was all too much. My mind was nearly numb from the stress.

About fifteen minutes later Carol stopped by again, this time with her two friends, Pam and Arlene.

"I wasn't going to leave you alone, Hassanain," Carol boldly announced. "You're suppose to be enjoying your time here. Besides, you don't think we are going to let you starve, do you?"

It appeared that I didn't have much say in the matter, for I soon found myself being dragged into the dining room. Reluctant though I was, I went, knowing that anything was better than being alone in my grim state of mind.

The three girls saw to it that I ate and, taking advantage of the free time which was then scheduled, they took me outside where others were involved in various winter sports. I discovered for the first time what skating, sledding, and tobogganing were all about. I enjoyed the activities very much and quite naturally found my distressing thoughts subsiding. This diversion proved to be a great relief.

Later I attended one of the seminars being held that evening. It so happened that the topic of the seminar was about how a Christian may nurture a closer walk with God—a subject which hardly interested me at the time. I decided to spend the rest of the evening by myself, for I had much to think about.

A cloud descended upon me again and lingered on through the night. Sleep would not come to me. Through the mist of my plaguing thoughts the Quran and my family remained etched vividly on my mind. I prayed to Allah. I asked him for help. I implored him to calm my troubled heart.

Throughout the following morning I remained secluded from everyone else. I was beginning to waver in my Muslim faith and I resolved to do something about it. I would not allow myself to fall away from Islam and bring shame and discredit to my family. True, I had come to see Christianity in a new light, but I was as determined as ever to cling to my faith.

I would cleave tenaciously to the Quran. It was my Holy Book. I had learned to recite it in Arabic and had memorized long sections of its pages. Its beauty was alluring, its message was captivating. I loved it. To discard the Quran was unthinkable.

I had decided. I must break off all contact with Christians and immerse myself once again in the Quran. Only then could I deal with the questions and doubts which gnawed away at me.

That afternoon I approached Carol to inform her of my decision. "I've come to realize what my problem is," I told her, hesitantly. "I guess I just don't want to be around Christians anymore. It's bothering me too much. I need to get away by myself in order to devote myself to my own faith without any hindrances. Be sure to tell Pam and Arlene and the others, will you, please?"

"I think I understand, Hassanain. Do what you think is best. I have certainly enjoyed getting to know you and learning something about your faith. Maybe we'll see each other again sometime."

"Who knows, maybe." I replied. "I'd like to tell you, Carol, that I really appreciate your friendship. You and Pam and Arlene are great people—but I need to do what I've told you. Thanks for everything."

It was not easy telling Carol that. She had been a good friend—that is, to the extent that I had known her. She was by no means a girl friend, or anything approaching it. It was just that she was so sincere in her convictions about her faith and in her concern for others. It was this sincerity that so appealed to me. There was nothing superficial about Carol. Although I had treated her rudely and scoffed at her beliefs not a few times, she continued to love and accept one of such a different faith as mine. This is what impressed me the most. Still, I could not figure out why she never shared her faith with me.

"Why don't you ever tell me about Jesus?" I finally asked.

"Why, would you like to know about him?" Carol inquired.

"No, no. Why is it that you don't tell me about Christianity like other people do? I'm constantly hearing that I have to become a born-again Christian. How come you never tell me this?"

"I've thought of it, Hassanain, but God hasn't led me to, so I never have. But I pray all the time that God will take care of you and that someday you will become a Christian."

"Well, Carol," I responded, reflecting for a moment on what she had said, "I'm going to miss all of you. I really am. I'd like you to sign my autograph book for me. Would you?"

"I surely will. I'd be honored to," came the eager reply.
And this is what she wrote:

Hassanain,
I really am glad I could get to know you and learn so
much about your past life. If you never remember
anything else, there's one thing I really want you to
remember: Jesus has changed my life, and I know he
can change yours. That may sound kinda strange but it's
really true, I know I could never make it through life
without him.

My thoughts and prayers will always be with you, that
maybe someday you will accept him as your Savior too.

Love,
Carol G.

ELEVEN
SURPRISED BY JOY

The note from Carol was very touching, but I was determined to see that her prayers would never be answered. I did not like the idea of having to end all but occasional contacts with my Christian friends, but I knew it was necessary for my own protection. I had to guard my faith.

I studied the Quran with a new vigor. No longer did I use only the Arabic text because, although I could pronounce its words, I could not entirely understand its meaning. So I began using an English translation in order to search more deeply into the message of my sacred book, the Quran.

In my effort to establish a defense for my faith I found some passages from the Quran which I thought would be good to use in a counter-attack against the Christians. What was happening to me during these days was all very strange. Think of it: I, who was firmly convinced of the truth of Islam, was having to seclude myself that I might bolster the defenses of my own faith. Why was it that I had to draw back in the first place? Why could I not simply rest in the knowledge that my faith was true? What was there for me to worry about? Yet there was a subtle uneasiness about this whole endeavor to buttress myself against Christianity.

Previously I had been intent on learning about the Christian faith in order to lead my friends to Islam. Now I was having to retreat to sustain my own faith. It was a strange turn of events indeed, and something I was not unaware of at the time.

To enhance my study of the Quran I consulted several Muslim publications about Islam which gave me new insights into many of the traditions and teachings of my faith. Often I would discuss my findings with my brother Mohammed and would ask him how I could most effectively argue against Christianity. Throughout these studies I would pray to Allah for guidance and help, knowing that ultimately only he could strengthen my faith.

Although I was glad that my time alone was serving its purpose well, I missed the friendship and vitality and enthusiasm I had experienced at Campus Life. From time to time I would call Carol or Pam to see how they were doing. On one such occasion at the end of March, Carol's brother, Steve, answered the phone.

"I suppose you're calling for Carol?" Steve remarked after we had talked for a few minutes.

"Yes, I am," I responded. "Is she home?"

"I think she's uptown shopping with Pam. They're getting ready for Campus Life's spring retreat next weekend. Are you planning to go, Hass?"

"I hadn't heard about it, but it sounds interesting. I'll tell you what. Have Carol call me back, will you?"

The next day I received a phone call from Wendell Amstutz.

"How are you doing, ol' buddy," he addressed me in his usual congenial way. "I've been thinking about you lately and I thought I'd call to see how you are. What's happening?"

"Not much. I'm managing to keep myself busy, though. I hear you're getting ready for a retreat?"

"We sure are and you're invited to come. We'd like to have you along."

"Well, I'll have to think about it. Thanks anyway," I said, not wanting to commit myself.

"Hass, the main reason I'm calling is that I'd like to get together with you sometime to talk. What do you think?"

"It's all right with me," I replied without a second thought. I had always respected Wendell, both as a Christian and as a leader of Campus Life. He was a good man, full of integrity, and forever willing to lend a helping hand. Like Carol, Pam, and Arlene, he accepted me as I was—a dedicated Muslim—and never tried to force me to become a Christian. I knew that for whatever reason Wendell wanted to get together I could look forward to a pleasant time with him. "When would you like to meet?" I asked.

"I'm going to be very busy over the next few days, so how about sometime right after the retreat. I'll call you up and we can arrange something then," Wendell answered, obviously pleased.

"Sounds good. I'll look forward to hearing from you," I ended, somewhat curious as to what was on his mind.

Later that same day Carol returned my call from the day before.

"I hear you've been shopping. What's going on?" I inquired.

"Just getting ready to go on our spring retreat. Are you going? It's with Campus Life."

"Well, I don't know. In a way I feel like it, but I'm not too sure. It would be nice to take a break and get away for the weekend. Life's been pretty monotonous the past few months."

"That's not a bad idea, Hassanain. All the people you know from Campus Life will be there. I'm sure they would be glad to see you again. I know you'd have a good time."

"You seem excited. Where is it, and what exactly is it all about?" I questioned.

"The weekend of activities will be very similar to the conference we had at the Marriott Inn last December, only this time we're having our retreat at Northwestern College. Northwestern is in the Twin Cities area, not too far from where you live, Hassanain. It's a fantastic place to have a retreat. The campus is heavily wooded and is next to two lakes—it's beautiful. Knowing you, I think you'd like it."

"I'll think about it, Carol. I just don't know right now. I want to pray about it first," I responded, cautiously.

"Okay. It has been good talking with you, Hassanain. I'll look forward to finding out what you decide. Good-bye."

I started to think the matter through. Wendell and Carol's invitation more than aroused my curiosity. With the advent of spring and the season change came also a desire for a change of pace. I had been a recluse long enough. I definitely did want to see my Campus Life friends again. "Surely I have added enough tenacity to my faith by this time," I reasoned to myself, "and, should the occasion arise, I should have no problem defending Islam. If someone approaches me to tell me what's what, I will have no difficulty silencing him. In fact, to any who may be interested, I should be able to give a convincing presentation of the truth of the Quran."

As I prayed about what to do, I began to think that God might have me go to the retreat as a witness, or representative, for Islam. My faith had matured considerably over the past three months and I felt that perhaps this time I could persuade some of the Christians to become Muslims. More than anyone else, I wanted to win Carol to the faith of Mohammed, because I knew she would make an exceptionally fine Muslim since she was such a good person. Besides, she would not go to heaven if she remained a Christian. What a shame, I thought, for such an upright person to go to hell. I decided to go.

The campus of Northwestern College was indeed a beautiful sight. Tucked away between two lakes and amid acres of trees, it seemed as though it were a world to itself.

The singing of birds filled the fresh April air with the invigorating sounds of spring. It was an ideal place for a retreat. In the middle of a metropolitan area, one could withdraw from the world outside for a weekend of refreshment and relaxation to ponder the more important issues of life.

Campus Life's spring retreat was much the same as "The Living End," except on a smaller scale. I felt strange being in the presence of the Campus Life group again. I did not have the feeling of "belonging." It wasn't that I was not accepted—several students expressed their gladness that I was back among them. It was that our outlook on life, although so similar, was yet *so different.* It was that "something" which I had sensed all along. Their lives for the most part possessed a special savor, a certain kind of liveliness that was hard to pin down. And I knew that it was somehow linked to their faith. Simply being in their presence made me feel well. Now all of this was a very difficult puzzle to piece together. What was I to make of a false faith that bore such positive and wholesome fruit? One could not argue against it. It wasn't long before the seeds of frustration were again taking root.

By the end of the first workshop on Saturday morning, the same cloud of gloom engulfed me as it had at "The Living End" conference. But this time the struggle was more intense. I was scared but I didn't know why. I began reciting a number of Muslim prayers in my mind and trying to convince myself over and over again that Christianity could not be true. Though I didn't realize it then, God's hand was heavily upon me—and this time there would be no escape.

I had spoken with Carol a few times thus far, but after that first seminar I kept more or less to myself. Disillusioned, I found a comfortable couch in the beautiful orange hallway of Nazareth Hall and just sat there, thinking. While there, deep in thought, Wendell Amstutz came by and sat down beside me. In that typical, informal way of his, he greeted me, "Hi, buddy, how are you going?" Usually when Wendell and I talked about religion, he would calmly tell me about the Bible and what he believed and would listen patiently as I told him my beliefs. This time, however, he had something new to say.

"You know, Hass," he continued, "last December at the Marriott Inn I sensed that you were being torn between two religions."

"Not really," I interrupted, not wanting to admit it.

"Well, this is why I called the other day to see if we could arrange a time to get together. I wanted to talk this over with you. Hass, do you want to know something? This weekend it has been on my mind continually that you will not leave this retreat or this college campus without first becoming a Christian. I definitely sense within my heart that God is telling me that you are going to accept Christ this weekend."

I laughed. "You must be kidding," I retorted, jokingly.

"No. I really believe God is going to do this."

"I doubt it," I said sarcastically. "That's what you may think, but I know better. There's no way! The way you guys believe about Christ, he is like a devil, Satan. We'll see."

"Well, buddy, you've got me a little perplexed now that you respond like this. I'd like to have a word of prayer with you before I go. Is that okay with you?"

"Sure, fine," I replied, for lack of anything else to say.

Wendell's prayer, what I remember of it, went as follows: "Hass has been a good friend, Lord, and I know you have been speaking to me from your own heart that he will become a Christian this weekend. Lord Jesus, I am leaving him in your hands and I pray that you will be with him and guide him in all of his struggles. Father, help him to make the right decision." He closed in Jesus' name and walked away, pausing to turn around and add, "I'll be seeing you around, buddy. We're going to be playing some ball if you'd like to come out and join us."

"All right. I might show up. Thanks."

What could I say? Wendell had never shared his faith with me, when suddenly he comes and tells me that I'll be a Christian before the weekend is over. "Ha, no way! No way will I become a Christian. No chance!" I kept saying to myself as I tried to harden my heart. Wendell's comments only added iron to my resolve never to allow myself to succumb to any temptation to receive Christ. I remained seated on the sofa for awhile, thinking over what Wendell had said. It really bothered me.

The same painful frustrations were coming over me as at the Marriot Inn three months before. I lifted myself from the couch and began to walk. I was headed nowhere in particular. I just had to get up and move about. I strolled around the campus from one end to another, back and forth, indoors and outdoors, for hours. I walked by the lake, up hills, across the grass, down long corridors, all the while trying my best to evade what would not leave me. I felt a summons from Christ, but I kept my ears covered. In defense, I brought to the fore the resources of my past months of study. But my efforts to vindicate Islam seemed futile. My strenuous attempt to suppress Christ was to no avail. He lingered on.

Finally, about two o'clock in the morning, I made my way to my room and went to bed. I just lay there motionless, unable to sleep, seeming to be imprisoned alone in a deep, dark dungeon where only harassing, tormenting thoughts were allowed to enter. I was greatly relieved when the darkness of the night passed and morning came. Seeing the brilliant beams of light bursting through the windows lifted my spirits.

I doubt if many can comprehend the kind of agony I was undergoing at the time. It was the background from which I was coming that made my struggle so acute. For years I was committed wholeheartedly to the belief that Islam is true. This belief was the bedrock of my life. However, this foundation was not only intellectual. It

included my passions, my will, my culture, my family; in
short, my life—everything. Few people are committed to
something so unreservedly. Therefore, when challenged
by something different, few encounter struggles so severe.
My foundation was beginning to crumble.

Everyone is devoted to something. God has somehow
created man such that he needs and seeks a "master."
And man will find a master, whether it be the true and
living God, his own lusts—sexual, financial greed, etc.—
another human being, a false religion, or whatever. No
man is completely without purpose. He has some reason
for living. There is some point around which his life
revolves. There is some purpose upon which his life
focuses, at least to a degree. If this were no not so, I suppose
most people would kill themselves out of despair.

If that which is the focal point of one's life is in jeopardy,
that person will accordingly be faced with a real crisis.
The lives of many people are based on matters so
inconsequential that the removal of these things causes little
dismay. The crucial factor in this context is not what
one holds most dear, but the degree to which he is
committed or involved with this reason for living. To the
degree that one is tied to this "master," to that same
degree one will struggle and suffer when it is threatened.

My life was Islam. For years it had stood as uncontested
truth. What troubled me about Christianity was that it
also had a claim on truth. And the consequence of rejecting
one at the acceptance of the other was eternal punishment
in the next life. Most people confronted by the claims of
Christ have not made a prior commitment to Islam, nor
do they come from a background which insists emphatically
that for them to become a Christian means a sure place
in hell. It was no little matter. Previously, of course, in
ignorance I had easily shrugged Christianity aside. But
no longer did I see it as the misguided religion of the West
which had been superseded by Mohammed and the Quran.
Christianity was altogether different than I, as a Muslim,

had been led to believe. The tables had turned and it was Islam that was now seen as lacking.

That morning I sought out Carol. I had to talk. But when I found her she told me she couldn't at the moment. "I can't talk with you now," Carol explained, "because I'm leaving to have a time alone with God. But I'll be happy to speak with you later." Discouraged, I went and sat in the same place I had been sitting the day before.

It wasn't a half-hour before Carol came and sat down beside me. Warmly, she said, "Hassanain, will you forgive me for not talking with you when you asked me?" Her thoughtful eyes revealed that she meant what she said. She explained that after hearing the retreat's main speaker give a message it was scheduled that everyone was to have a "quiet time" alone with the Lord. "I know I said 'no' when you came to me," Carol went on, "but I'll tell you one thing, I was praying for you the whole time."

Pleased to hear this, I noticed that Pam and Arlene, who were sitting on the next sofa, stood up and walked away. Unknown to me then, they too were leaving for their rooms to pray for me.

"Carol," I said, "I've been tossing about many things in my mind lately." Her face softly saddened as a few tears began trickling down her cheeks. "Why are you crying?" I asked.

"Hassanain, I remember when you asked me why I never shared my faith with you. Well, I'm going to now because, while I was alone praying, God sent me out here to speak with you. I must share some things with you. Do you want me to do this?"

"You might as well," I said with a sigh. "Everyone else does."

Before she began telling me about Christ, she asked me some questions about Islam. Among other things, she asked if I thought I would go to heaven if I died that day.

"Of course," I declared arrogantly, defending myself to the bitter end, "I do my five daily prayers, fast, and

everything else. I'll go to heaven, I'm certain of it."
Naturally, since no Muslim can be sure of this, I wasn't
either, but I did not want to admit it.

"That's good to hear," Carol remarked, seemingly
happy. "God has given us many promises in the Bible,"
she continued, undaunted. "The greatest is John 3:16: 'For
God so loved the world that he gave his only begotten
Son that whoever believes in him shall not perish but have
eternal life.' "

I had heard this passage so many times that I had it
memorized. But I listened carefully, I didn't disagree or
raise any objections. For once I didn't feel like arguing back,
so I remained still and attentive as Carol explained what
a person must do and understand to become a Christian.

"Hassanain, you believe as the Bible teaches that 'all
have sinned and fall short of the glory of God' (Rom. 3:23),
and that because of this we all stand in need of God's
forgiveness. But you must understand that forgiveness does
not come about by doing a series of religious good works.
In Romans it says, 'For the wages of sin is death, but the
gift of God is eternal life in Christ Jesus our Lord' (6:23).
Hassanain, this means that God offers salvation to us
freely. In other words, forgiveness is a gift offered by God
which it is our responsibility to receive. John tells us
that 'He,' that is Christ, 'came to that which was his own,
but his own did not receive him. Yet to all who received
him, to those who believed in his name, he gave the right to
become children of God' (1:11, 12). Receiving Christ,
Hassanain, is taking him as your own Savior from sin. It's
like inviting him into your life. Jesus said, 'Here I am!
I stand at the door and knock. If anyone hears my voice and
opens the door, I will go in and eat with him, and he with
me' (Rev. 3:20). You see, Christ stands at the door of
your life and asks to come in. But you must open the door
and let him in. When you do, He will come in and
fellowship with you." It was very beautiful how she quoted

and explained these passages from the Bible to me. It was clear and meaningful.

Carol told me that the main reason she was sad was because of all that I had gone through in Uganda and was now going through in my struggles with religion. "I know you are experiencing a great deal of pressure and strain," she said, "but the Bible says that God will take all of your burdens upon himself and give you abundant life in their place. Jesus said, 'I came that they might have life, and might have it abundantly' (John 10:10, NASB)."

"What do you mean by abundant life?" I questioned.

"Abundant life means that God will take care of your problems. I'm not saying you won't have any troubles in life. You will have problems, but you can share them with God. Here, let me give you this verse," she continued as she paged through her Bible. " 'No temptation has seized you except what is common to man. And God is faithful; he will not let you be tempted beyond what you can bear. But when you are tempted, he will also provide a way out so that you can stand up under it' (1 Cor. 10:13). Hassanain, I want you to be happy and the only way I know how you can be is by receiving Jesus Christ into your life."

I don't know what came over me at the time, but my mind was in an absolute daze. I did not know what to think anymore. My whole body was beginning to shake. I could no longer argue or defend myself. I was helpless. It would be impossible to describe what was going on within me. My mind was a chaos of swirling, confused thoughts. Bleakness.

"Would you like to accept Christ as your Savior now, Hassanain?" Carol asked.

I said nothing. I couldn't.

"I'll say a prayer for you," she went on, "All you have to do is repeat the words after me." She started to pray, but I remained quiet. When she had finished the prayer I still hadn't spoken. There were a few moments of silence, and then, without pressing me any further, she said, "I'll really be praying for you, Hassanain, because I think you are a very good person, but yet you need Jesus. Everybody needs Jesus."

A few minutes passed by, neither one of us moving or saying anything. Then my mind began to clear and, in a forlorn, cheerless sort of voice, I uttered, "No matter what religion is the right one, there is only one God. O God," I implored, "I don't know who I am talking to right now, but whoever you are, show me the right way."

Again there was silence. My mind drifted back into a blank. But soon into the void came an image of the Quran —a very vivid image, as if to say, "This is *the* Book." After the Quran came my family—each member passing before my mind, as clear and distinct as though I were actually in their presence. It was the Adversary's last call before he lost me. I writhed in torment. It was all too much. "O God," I cried, "please show me the way." Over and over again I repeated this. Suddenly, somehow, I told Carol to repeat the prayer. I don't know how or why I ever said this. It just came out of my mouth. Startled, Carol looked at me slightly surprised, almost unbelieving. "Could this really be?" she seemed to wonder.

"Okay—okay," said Carol as she bowed her head. I noticed tears coming from her eyes again.

"Dear Lord Jesus," came the gentle voice, saying slowly and very carefully to allow me time to repeat: "I open the door of my life to you and I invite you into my heart. I ask you to come and take over my life and forgive all the sins I have committed. I pray that from now on I will do everything that is according to your will."

With my head bowed and my eyes closed I repeated every word out loud as if it were my own. As I prayed, graphic portrayals of the Quran and the faces of every member of my family kept sweeping through my mind. My body was shaking and my voice was cracking as I forced

each word out of my mouth. It was so hard to pray this
prayer, yet there was another power enabling me to say it.
I could have stopped at any point—especially when I saw
the faces of my beloved family—but something else kept
me going.

"Jesus," I continued after Carol, "I thank you that you
have *already* come into my life and that you have
already forgiven my sins just as you have promised." As I
prayed these words of thanksgiving, full of faith that what
I was saying was true, an unspeakable joy began to blossom
forth within me until it flooded my entire being. It was a
joy I'd never known existed. And with it came a
transcending peace which dispelled all fear of what might
come upon me as a result of yielding to the risen Christ.
Jesus, the sovereign Lord, enveloped me in a love so
overwhelming that I was assured of his very presence. I
knew I was weak in myself and my assurance rested not
on any determination or stubborn will of my own, but on a
quiet peace which came from God.

Carol wept for joy. She cried so loudly that I was sure
she could be heard throughout the building. She fumbled
around for her handkerchief, but couldn't manage to find it.
Finally, she had to settle for holding her hands to her eyes
to catch the flow of tears.

Seeing her, I wept also. I felt so free. A tremendous
burden had been lifted from me. As a Muslim I had been
very happy. I had one of the most beautiful of families.
There was no sadness in my life other than losing my father
and, of course, Uganda. But the joy which Christ gave me
was much richer, much deeper than any happiness I had
ever known—it surpassed even the bitter despondency,
which, as a result of my spiritual struggles, had preceded it.

Collecting herself, Carol said, "You know something,
Hassanain? I just praise the Lord because you've been on
my prayer list for a long, long time. Now at last I can take
that list off my wall and thank God for answering my
prayers. Up till now every prayer was answered except for

you. I never knew if this would happen. I could never say you'd become a Christian—not you. You were too strong in your faith. But I'm glad you did, because I think you've made the right decision. Let's go tell everyone about it!"

I was not quite so enthusiastic, for instantly Wendell Amstutz came to mind. Because of what I had said the day before he was the last person on earth I wanted to tell. Oh, how I didn't want to face him! For some reason he hadn't crossed my mind till now. The mere thought of him embarrassed me.

As we stood up from the sofa, about to leave to announce the good news, I said soberly, "Carol, do you know what is going to happen to me when my family finds out I'm a Christian?"

"I know it will be hard, Hassanain, but God will give you the same strength to tell them as he gave you to accept Christ."

"But there is *no way* I can tell my family," I objected, not willing to believe Carol, yet finding it impossible not to.

"Well, you don't have to. The Lord will," Carol insisted as we slowly walked away.

"I'm sure he's going to go home and tell my family, 'Hassanain is a Christian now,' " I replied, desperately trying to avoid thinking of the inevitable.

"You know he has the power to do that, but he can also use you to tell your family. God will give you the strength when the time comes. Don't worry."

While we were talking, I glanced down and noticed the marble tie pin which I was wearing that said in Arabic, "Allah." I took it off. I did not want to see it again—it was over, finished.

As we continued down the hall, we stopped to talk to other students along the way. Then, as we walked a little further, to my dismay, we came across Wendell Amstutz. My heart sank. What was I going to say?

"Oh . . . a . . . Wendell . . . ." Carol began with a broad smile.

Without saying a word, Wendell held his hand up toward Carol and shook his head, motioning her to stop. He came up to me, put his arms around me, and after a moment's silence said, "God bless you, brother. Welcome to the family." That's all. He already knew I was a Christian! He never said, "I told you so," as I'd expected him to say. There was no embarrassment, no explanations—just friendship.

It was Palm Sunday, April 7, 1974. As Jesus so triumphantly entered Jerusalem nearly two millennia before, he likewise came into my life, hailed as King. It was a joyous memorable day, but yet tinged with a relentless gnawing of fear.

I had yet to inform my family.

TWELVE
AFTERMATH

The exuberance of those first hours was short-lived.
Wendell offered me a ride home from the retreat and while
on our way I revealed my apprehension about the future. I
was content, peaceful with my decision to give myself to
Christ, but yet I was restless and uneasy about what lay
ahead. I feared what would happen when I told my family.
They would not take it lightly—I knew that. To hear that I
had become a Christian would pierce their hearts deeply
and perhaps create an unbridgeable chasm between us. I
told Wendell how much I loved my family and how I
dreaded to hurt them.

Wendell did his best to encourage me. He told me to pray
that God would prepare my family to accept what I had
done and that God would give me the strength and wisdom
to tell them at the appropriate time. The prayers of many,
Wendell affirmed reassuringly, would be supporting me.

I delayed the announcement for a few days to give me
time to collect myself, think matters through, and to pray.
I didn't have the slightest notion as to how I should
make the news known, so I asked God continually for the
wisdom to know how to deal with the situation. I could not
draw strength or comfort from the Bible which Carol

had given me, for I had hidden it in the basement to avoid detection for the time being. I was tempted occasionally to read the Quran, which still lay by my bed, but I brushed the thought aside. I even wondered at times if being a Christian was worth the price I knew I might very well have to pay. I could not imagine a greater loss than that of losing my family. I prayed much, therefore, for the necessary strength to cope with the confrontation that was yet to come.

By Wednesday, three days after the retreat, I knew the time had come. My allegiance to Christ could remain hidden no longer. I called Wendell, Carol, and others to inform them that I would be speaking with my family and asked them to pray for me. Frightened and restless with anxiety, yet trusting God to see me through, I called Rahanna into my bedroom. I would tell her first and ask her to spread the news to the others.

"*Bhabi,*" I said solemnly, addressing her as always with the proper title for a sister-in-law, "this past weekend I became a Christian."

She paused, and, frowning in displeasure, began to walk away. She didn't believe me.

"*Bhabi,* I really mean it. I have become a Christian."

Rahanna turned, her sullen countenance changing to a grim scowl. "You mean this weekend? Is that what you were doing?"

"Yes."

"That's *kafir* (blasphemy)."

In her view becoming a Christian was like turning over one's life to Satan, so I replied, "No, I'm not a *kafir,* neither have I accepted a *kafir.* Jesus is my Savior and Lord."

"Hassanain," came her trembling, yet angry voice, "do you realize what you have done? How could you do this to your family? How will you tell your mother and brothers? You know your mother is not strong, and yet you do something like this?"

"I have turned this whole matter over to God. I am

praying that he will help each of you to accept what I have done. I'd like you to tell the rest of the family for me. Would you, please?"

Shocked and dismayed, she said she would and left the room. I knelt at my bed and prayed about what lay immediately before me. It would not be easy.

A few minutes passed, then I heard a cry that rang throughout the house. "Hassanain," came my mother's hysterical voice, and then another, more desperate, "Hassanain!" My foremost fear had come to pass. Nothing in life could hurt me more than the thought of grieving my mother. Reluctantly, I walked toward the door. I did not want to leave my room, but I knew I had to face her.

Mother was shaking and weeping loudly when I approached her. "How could you do that?" she asked, looking at me dismally through her tear-filled eyes. "You are a *kafir's* son now" (not her son anymore).

This struck deeply into my heart. I was having to bear the unbearable. Perhaps no mother ever loved a son so dearly—and now I was no longer her own, but the devil's child. Yet I could empathize with her for I knew her feelings. A few days before, I shared her thoughts about Christianity. It was terribly difficult for her.

She began yelling at me and striking her hands against her head. Finally she couldn't say a word and broke down and wept bitterly. I tried to comfort her but to no avail. About fifteen minutes passed, when Mohammed, returning from a nearby park with his daughter, walked through the door. Staring at his sobbing wife and mother he turned to me with a questioning, troubled look.

"Hassanain has become a Christian," Rahanna murmured.

"What!" Mohammed yelled at the top of his voice as he moved towards me. Grabbing my shirt with both hands near the collar he shouted, "Do you know what you are doing?"

"Yes, I do," I replied, saying nothing further until he

began pushing me around, then I exclaimed, "I have accepted Jesus Christ. The Quran says there is an age at which I can choose what to believe."

"But you're not old enough yet," Mohammed answered angrily. "How can you say that when you don't know enough about Islam? You have made the wrong choice. Why don't you think about it first?"

Mohammed was furious. His frustration overflowed into tears as he shoved me into a chair. Beside himself with rage and grief, he began choking me. Overcome by intense sorrow, he burst into a frenzy of wailing and weeping. I honestly don't think he realized what he was doing.

I don't know where Hanif had been, but suddenly he came into the picture and rushed to my aid, only to be whisked aside by Mohammed. However, he intervened again and somehow I managed to get away.

I had to leave the house. I couldn't tolerate all the crying any longer, especially my mother's. It sounded as if I was attending my own funeral.

As I headed toward the door, Mohammed called out to me, "As long as you've found your own God, find your own place!" My bitterest dream had now come true—I was disowned by my own family.

The next thing I knew I was tumbling backwards down the front steps. I picked myself up and found my New Testament, which, in the event I should be told to leave, I had hidden outside earlier in the day. Again and again I glanced behind me at the house as I walked away. I was overwhelmed by a piercing sense of desolation. I was tasting the first sip of the cup of grief I was to drink for many months.

I opened my New Testament at random to receive some word of consolation. My eyes fell on James 1:2: "Dear brothers, is your life full of difficulties and temptations? Then be happy . . ." (TLB). Immediately I closed the Bible and began thumping it against my knee as I walked along. "I'm sure!" I fumed, irritated by what I had read. "How can I be happy when I've just been expelled from my own home?" I reasoned to myself. "By believing in Christ, I have deeply hurt my mother. I can never be happy!"

Exasperated, I exclaimed, "Well, Jesus, is this what I get for accepting you? Where is this 'abundant life' I'm supposed to get?" Had I been willing to yield my situation to God and trust him completely that he knew what he was doing in my life, I would never have gotten angry at him. God, being forever faithful, was willing to provide the compassion and understanding I needed at the time, but I refused to receive it. It would be a few weeks before I would surrender everything entirely to God's will.

I trudged to a nearby telephone booth and called the pastor of the Lutheran church which had sponsored our resettlement in America. "I've just told my family that I've become a Christian and now I can no longer stay at home," I explained. The pastor already knew I was a Christian for I had told him within the past three days.

"We thought that might happen, Hass, so we've prepared a place for you to stay tonight at the home of one of our church members." With a keen sense of relief, I felt as though I had just been given a cool, refreshing drink on a hot, weary day. I went for a little walk, called Carol to tell her my circumstances, then went to the church a block away to see the pastor. It wasn't long before I arrived at the home where I stayed for the night—and, for that matter, for the next three months.

That evening I received a phone call from my mother, who was calling on behalf of Mohammed. My family, not easily daunted, had gotten in touch with me by obtaining my phone number from the Lutheran pastor. Mohammed had a proposal for me.

"I want you to think this whole matter through," he began as he took the phone, still weeping profusely. "You need to know more about Islam. You know little about it now. We will put all our money together—if we have to we'll live on dry bread—but we want to send you to holy

Mecca so that you can see what Islam is really like. Then you can make your decision."

It was more than a kind gesture. My family was truly prepared to sacrifice to the limit to get me to Mecca in the hope that I would return to Islam. At the moment I didn't want to oppose Mohammed so I simply said I would think about it. I had caused him enough agony as it was.

But that was not good enough for Mohammed. Infuriated, he replied, "What's there to think about?" And, in a flurry of anger, he began yelling at me and hung up the phone.

Needless to say, the weeks and months which followed were extremely hard for me. Perhaps no one who has never had to face the anguish of such loss can comprehend even remotely the extent of the sadness I felt in those days. The absence of my family left a tremendous aching void in my life. Had I not loved them immensely, I would never have experienced such a terrible emptiness without them.

Wendell, Carol, and my friends at Campus Life were very encouraging to me, as were the pastor and people of West Bloomington Evangelical Free Church where I began attending regularly. Whenever I became discouraged, the kindness and understanding extended to me by these people would inspire me to continue steadfastly in the faith.

About six weeks after I became a Christian, Youth for Christ/Campus Life sponsored a fund-raising banquet at Soul's Harbor, a large church in downtown Minneapolis. Before a large gathering of pastors and Christian youth workers throughout the area, several other students and I shared how God had used Campus Life's ministry in our lives.

Beginning with my years in Uganda, I told everyone of God's working in my life. For the first time since becoming a Christian I caught a glimpse of my life as a whole. I saw that God's hand had been on me from the very beginning. He had been the Engineer and Architect of my life, designing each episode to find its place in keeping with his ultimate purpose to rescue me "from the domain of darkness and [transfer me] to the kingdom of His beloved Son" (Col. 1:13, NASB). Overwhelmed with a sense of awe at what God had done in my life, I told the audience that all the glory was to be to Christ. I asked everyone to pray for those of my family, for Christ had yet to make himself known to them.

What I had to say seemed to have affected many people, for several approached me afterwards to arrange various speaking engagements. But whatever they may have gained from hearing my story, I was greatly encouraged from the renewed awareness that Christ was indeed Lord of my life. God had ministered *to me* behind that podium. I knew that even the clarity of mind with which I spoke came from the touch of God's grace.

The several speaking opportunities which grew out of that evening were what really kept me going in my Christian life in the weeks which followed. Having to take a public stand for Christ strengthened the fiber of my faith, in addition to providing an added incentive to deepen my understanding of the Scriptures. But there was another side to that first night of speaking. The overview of my life which I saw brought back many treasured memories of my family—from the early years, through the crisis in Uganda, to our journey to the United States. Now I found myself again having to contend with the agonizing emptiness I sensed at their loss.

Shortly after speaking at the Youth for Christ banquet, my sister Zehra, together with her family, came to visit us from Tanzania. I hadn't seen Zehra for more than two years. She'd left us after her marriage, about eight months before we fled Uganda. I longed to see her again, but I didn't take it upon myself to do so until my mother invited me home to see her about three weeks after her arrival in America.

With a joy tinged with sorrow, my sister and I greeted each other with a hug. How long it had been since we had last seen one another! All our years together in Kampala raced across my mind. My heart ached as I felt her tears fall on me.

"You finally lost," Zehra said, in a quiet, somber voice, referring to the many times we used to quiz each other on the Quran.

"No," I replied softly, yet confidently, "I won." She said nothing in reply. I don't know what she was thinking. But within me my heart throbbed for them. I longed for them to allow Christ to embrace them as he had so firmly embraced me.

On one occasion, while reading my Bible, I discovered that I belonged to the "family of God." With God as our Father, I was to consider all true Christians as brothers and sisters. This, though fascinating and very comforting, still could not quite replace the natural familial ties which members of a close-knit family enjoy among themselves. Often I found myself torn between loyalty to Christ and loyalty to my family. Yet God's grace was always sufficient to see me through these trying times. The passage which Carol shared with me kept coming to mind: "No temptation has seized you except what is common to man. And God is faithful; he will not let you be tempted beyond what you can bear. But when you are tempted, he will also provide a way out so that you can stand up under it" (1 Cor. 10:13). I thought of Jesus' words: "Come to me, all you who are weary and burdened, and I will give you rest" (Matt. 11:28). I would picture myself going to him, and leaning against him, yielding my heaviness of heart to him.

From time to time my mother would call and either she or Mohammed would ask me if I was interested in their offer to go to Mecca. "No," I would tell them, "I have made up my mind. I will remain a Christian." Despite this, about two months after I left home, Mother asked me to return for a visit so she could see me again. When I came to the door she joyfully exclaimed, "Oh, my son, you came," and, as the tears flowed freely, we greeted each other with warm, cheerful hugs. That she called me her son is a cherished memory. Not long before, she told me I was the devil's son. She fed me well and, as always, treated me very kindly. The entire time I was home, four or five hours, no one else spoke to me.

Nevertheless, with the passing of time, my fractured relationship with my family began to heal. By the middle of winter they asked me to return home to stay on the condition that I not interfere with their faith nor they with mine.

Of course, I missed them a great deal and wanted to be back with them again, but I knew that such a move would not be without its problems. However, I had lived in several places since leaving home and was tired of continually moving, so I decided to accept their offer.

Naturally, they were hoping that my moving in with them would eventually bring me back to Islam. And I thought that by so doing I would be showing them that even though I had turned away from their faith, I had not turned away from them. I still loved them and I did not want them to think that because I had accepted Christ I had, in effect, rejected them.

Although I immensely enjoyed being with my family again, I soon realized that it would be a strain on my newfound faith. I wasn't able to fellowship with other Christians as much as I needed and my study of the Bible was hampered considerably. After four months I made arrangements with my good friend Aaron Bundsieke to move into an apartment with him. My family had done nothing to prompt me to leave home. I just felt that under the circumstances it was the wisest thing to do.

Because it was my own decision to move, my mother was very grieved. Undoubtedly, she assumed that I had lost interest in the family and no longer cared about them. It disturbed me greatly, knowing that they could not understand why I left home. And, as a result, I began to suffer my severest temptations to return to my former Islamic way of life.

My faith was being tested considerably during these days and, though I didn't question the truth of Christianity, I would sometimes waver in my Christian commitment. At times I felt as though I were adrift on a storm-tossed sea. I felt a tremendous pull towards the life I left. Islam, as a way of life, intricately bound up with the family, was a powerful and compelling force which vied with my continued allegiance to Christ.

At one point I was on the precipice of again becoming a Muslim. I decided in an instant to relinquish all and again return to my family and Islam. I sprang from my chair and headed for the door. Suddenly, I stopped. I would glance at the Bible one last time—a sort of "farewell" to Christianity—then I would leave it and depart for home. I sat down again and flipped open the Bible. "Never will I leave you; never will I forsake you" (Heb. 13:5), I read, not knowing where I had turned. I felt like closing the book and hurrying off, but I was struck by the meaning of the passage and impelled to read it again.

As I pondered the implications of these words, it occurred to me with all the power and wonder and glory of a brilliant, rising sun that no matter how faithless I may be to Christ, he will remain ever faithful to me. I was in the palm of his hand and would remain so, forever. How futile it would be, then, to deny him. How senseless to flee such love, so "rich and pure, measureless and strong." Warmed by the flaming heart of Christ, I was stirred to a renewed sense of commitment.

Whenever I was shaken in my faith, Christ was always there to protect me. Thoughts of him would burst forth within me until he was more important than all else besides. A special awareness of his presence with me would overshadow all other concerns. God's promise that he would never leave me or forsake me has kept me faithful to him to this day.

THIRTEEN
FULLNESS OF LIFE

In May of 1975 an internationally distributed magazine
published an article about my life in Uganda and my
conversion to Christ. I was grateful for the opportunity to
share my experience of Christ's redeeming love through a
widely circulated magazine. I had high hopes that my
article would be read by many Muslims.

Early one morning that spring, my phone rang. An
unfamiliar male voice came from the other end. Clearly a
foreigner, the man asked me, "Is it true that you were a
Muslim and then became a Christian?"

"Yes," I replied, wondering what was on his mind.

"Well, I am a Muslim and have read your story in a
magazine. I am interested in hearing more about Christ—
maybe he is for me also. I have a lot of questions. Could
we meet this morning? I can pick you up shortly?"

"All right. I'll be happy to meet with you," I said, not
questioning whether or not the man was being sincere. I
gave the stranger my address and waited for him to stop by.
I prayed that God would direct my thoughts and words as
I told him about the Christian faith.

After picking me up in a car, the Muslim stranger, in his
mid-twenties, began asking me about Uganda. He told me

he was from Egypt, so we exchanged views about Africa, our native continent. Although I noticed a copy of the magazine containing my article lying on the front seat, he didn't seem interested in hearing about my faith in Christ.

When we came to Loring Park near downtown Minneapolis, the man parked the car. We had been together almost a half-hour and it did strike me as a little strange that our conversation had for the most part centered on Africa and not Christianity. I expected that once we found a quiet, secluded spot in the park we would begin to discuss our different faiths.

It was a quiet, peaceful morning. The bright green grass, damp with dew, glistened in the early morning sun. Beams of light shone through the trees, reflecting off the placid water of the park's pond. As I gazed across the grounds of the park, I could see that no one was present but us. It would be an ideal morning to visit alone with this inquisitive Egyptian Muslim.

"Let's get out," he suggested. "We can talk better outside." I opened the car door. Just as I stepped out, two other men instantly appeared in front of me. Where they had come from so suddenly I will never know. The two men, who appeared to be Muslim Arabs, grabbed me before I closed the door. One held onto me while the other beat me in the face and in the stomach until I fell to the ground, writing in pain. As I lay on my back, I saw all three men standing over me, staring down with cruel, hostile looks.

They each began kicking me until I just wanted to float into unconsciousness to ease the pain that racked my body. One of them yanked my head up by the hair and then jerked it to the ground again. Finally, as blood oozed out of my mouth and nose, they stopped kicking me.

A pencil and paper were thrust into my hands. "Deny Jesus right now!" came a harsh voice. "Write on this paper that you do not believe in Jesus, but rather Allah. Confess that you made a tragic mistake."

"I cannot do that," I said firmly.

"We will kill you, then. Allah commands it."

I saw a silver knife flash in the morning sun. One of the men bent down and held it to my throat. He said nothing as he pressed the sharp tip of the blade into my skin. "Renounce Christ now," he ordered, "or we will write it for you in your own blood after you are dead."

"You cannot kill a dead person," I replied.

"What do you mean?"

"I died the day I accepted Jesus Christ into my life," I said with conviction. That angered the knife-wielding Muslim even more and I felt the knife press closer. "If you want to kill me then go right ahead, because 'for me to live is Christ and to die is gain,'" I continued, without realizing at the time I was repeating the words of the Apostle Paul.

"You make no sense!" Two of them kicked me again while the other pulled me up by my shirt. He flashed the knife before me as a reminder of the seriousness of their threat to kill me. "You think this is all a joke, don't you," he said bitterly. "What Allah commands is no joke, and he commands that you renounce Christ or die. You are an apostate and a traitor to our people."

I closed my eyes as I silently prayed, "Please, Lord, you better do something or your body will be stabbed to death."

"What have you decided?" came the angry voice. "Will you confess in writing that you made a mistake?"

"No, I won't."

A school bell rang from across the street. Startled, the three men looked up. The one gripping my shirt and pressing the knife to my throat let go. My head hit the ground. All three of them stood over me again and muttered to themselves in Arabic as students from Metropolitan Junior College began pouring out of the school. I could hear voices and laughter which grew louder as some of the students headed for the park. With a few final swift kicks the men retorted, "We'll get you later, you apostate." They ran a few feet to the car and sped away.

I stumbled to my feet and sought help at a nearby hospital.

One day in July of the same year I went to beautiful Lake Nokomis in Minneapolis to spend an afternoon alone with God, praying to him and meditating upon his Word. The day was serene in all the splendor of midsummer Minnesota. A cool breeze gently swept across the lake as I sat under the spacious shade of a large oak tree. Sailboats seemed to dance lightly on the water as birds gaily swooped overhead. The day was manifest with all the good things in God's creation.

I spent much time reading my Bible and speaking with my Lord. Ours was a time of precious fellowship. The Father touched me with a special awareness of his presence as he made the Scriptures sing with life. My heart was warmed as I sensed the closeness and matchless love of the Incarnate God. The affection and joy and comfort of the Holy Spirit ran deep.

While reflecting on the greatness of God and pondering his involvement in my life, I tried to understand what the purpose was in the sorrow I experienced at the loss of my native Uganda and my beloved family. I began to wonder why God allowed me to go through all that I had. Why the loss of country and family—that which I held most dear?

In my reading, Jesus' words in Matthew 6:33 stood out to me in bold relief: "But seek first His kingdom and His righteousness, and all these things will be given to you as well." As I gave much thought to these words I realized afresh that God must be given first place in everything. He is worthy of nothing less than our wholehearted devotion—and he desires nothing less.

God knows the end to which he has created us and if he demands our all it is for our own good. He has made us— and wants us—to experience the fullness of life which can only be had by placing him at the center of our lives. But our affections are by nature always elsewhere. Sometimes we think we are seeking God when in reality we are only seeking the satisfaction or fulfillment of that need in our lives which we think God can provide. God wants to fulfill our needs, but in so doing he wants us to seek earnestly after him in the fullness of who he is. In other words, in some people's "search" for God, it is not God whom they actually seek, but some side effect or benefit which the "discovery" of God can provide. For example, some people desperately want peace of mind. They hear that Christ can provide such peace, so they seek Christ not for who he is in himself, but for the peace of mind he is able to give. God, however, wants us to desire *himself,* wholly and chiefly.

I suppose to a certain extent my experience as a Muslim was a groping after spiritual reality under the guise of seeking the true God. I thought I truly knew God, but as I strove to adhere to the stringent requirements of my faith, I doubt if I performed my religious duties out of a sincere love for God, but more than likely out of the satisfaction I gained in attaining my own "righteousness." This could easily result in a complacent and self-righteous attitude before God, degenerating into a reliance on one's own self-sufficiency and therefore really losing sight of God.

I do not believe that if God left us to ourselves, we would truly seek him wholeheartedly. We are drawn much too strongly to the things of this earth. But God in his love stoops down and intervenes in our lives, giving us trials that we might lose sight of ourselves and this fading world and seek to confide in him. God was showing me clearly that he wanted me completely, without reserve. And I came to realize that had I not lost what I held dearest—my native Uganda and my family—I would undoubtedly never have come to know the true and living God. I would have continued to cling to what is other than God. God—the true end and fulfillment in life—had allowed suffering so that my priorities in life in regard to him would be in their proper order.

Since I loved Christ more than all else and wanted him
to be supreme in my life, I rejoiced at the answer God
had given me that day. I would set my heart like a flint to
seek God and his righteousness and, come what may, I
would trust God that whatever he allowed to happen in my
life it would be for the ultimate fulfillment of this end.
My heart overflowed in thankgiving and appreciation at the
mercy and goodness of God which had so delicately guided
the events of my life. I had come to see that clearly his
kingdom and his righteousness are ultimately most
important.

And Christ has kept his promise that "all these things
[would] be given to [me] as well." Although he has not
returned me to the beauty of Africa's Uganda, he has
granted me citizenship in heaven whose gracious King is the
Lord Jesus Christ—the King of kings and Lord of lords
(Phil. 3:20). Like Abraham of old, I am now "looking
forward to the city with foundations, whose architect and
builder is God" (Heb. 11:10).

While attending Northwestern College to further my
knowledge of the Bible, I met the woman who was to
become my beloved wife. Together with our child, Shamim,
my wife Kathy and I seek to partake of the unity,
stability, and love which God intends for a Christian family.
Next to my salvation, my wife and child are the most
treasured of all God's gifts to me. Truly Christ's promise
has been fulfilled through his provision of such a beautiful
family.

God has given me fullness of life. He has transformed
sorrow into joy. My greatest moment was the time I gave my
life completely over to Christ. He has given me a joy and
a peace and an assurance that I had never known as a
Muslim. Jesus has set me free from a way of life dominated
by a religion of law. He has given me a richness of
fellowship with himself which infinitely transcends all that
I formerly cherished. By receiving Christian baptism I have
declared publicly my identification with Christ as Savior

and my resolve never to depart from his Lordship over me. To serve him in loving devotion is the aim of my life. I long to tell others, and especially my own Muslim people, of the love and grace of the Lord Jesus Christ and the good news that in him one can receive forgiveness of sin and eternal life.

FOURTEEN
TRUTH

When I was a Muslim, torn between belief in Islam and the Christ of the Bible, I knew that my struggle hinged on the question of truth. Concerning my view of God, I knew that if the Bible was true, then I, as a Muslim, was in the wrong. And I knew that ultimately nothing mattered more than one's relationship with God. Therefore, when I began to discover that my understanding of God was not the same as that of Christians, I realized that in all fairness I should attempt to acquaint myself with the Christian faith.

There are some key issues which I think are crucial to know about if people are to understand the differences between Islam and Christianity. These differences are important because they have to do with truth, and consequently with one's relationship to Christ, who is "the Truth."

Now the question of truth is one which strikes at the heart of the prevailing mentality of our generation. "Why," many ask, "should I bother myself over whether or not something is true? Is not the important question whether or not something is meaningful to me as I see it? Am I not the measure of all that is good and true and right? After all, what is good and true and right varies from individual to individual, does it not? So don't bother me with your 'truth.' I have my own. Your 'truth' may be fine for you, but it has no bearing on my life."

For many people the question of truth has become, for the most part, unimportant and irrelevant. Incredibly, in some circles the definition of truth has even seemed to change. Instead of meaning that which is opposed to what is false, "truth" has been twisted to mean whatever one finds most fulfilling in life or whatever is most meaningful. In other words, what is true for one person may not be true for another.

This pragmatic, relativistic view of life becomes most noticeable when we shift our attention to the realm of ethics. We are told never to pass judgment on another's beliefs or practices as long as they do not infringe on our own rights. The colloquial expressions "If it feels good, do it" and "Do your own thing" have become the moral guideposts of our day. What is right or wrong for one person may not be for another. As it is held that there is no absolute standard by which to decipher truth from falsehood, there is likewise none by which to judge moral conduct.

Strangely, when it comes to matters of religious faith, many people insist that we suspend the criterion of truth. Objections often heard are: One religion is just as good as another, so why try to change someone else's beliefs? It doesn't matter which religion is the correct one, because when it comes right down to it they're all the same, anyway.

Picture two men stranded in the middle of a desert. They have been lost for a week, their supplies have run out, and if they don't find help within a day they will collapse and die. Somehow they happen to come across an automobile whose gas tank is empty, but beside the car are two large fuel tanks. Each tank has a sign on it saying, "This is the correct fuel for the car." However, someone has left a note of instructions explaining that actually only one of the tanks contains gasoline for the car, while the fluid in the other tank will destroy the engine. The tanks are designed so that no one can examine their contents to find out which contains the correct fuel. Once one tank is opened the other will be automatically sealed for good, so it is necessary that they choose the right tank the first time. Although the note does not state which tank contains the correct fuel, it does say that there is a certain clue, which, if the men think hard enough, they should be able to discover. The instructions also say that there is a map in the car showing the way to safety which can be reached with the car.

The men inspect the automobile and the fuel tanks and find things just as the note explains. Now they must decide which tank they should open. They discuss the matter at length and are still not able to unlock the clue, but they think they have made some headway in finding which tank has the gasoline. In a situation like this, imagine the men shrugging their shoulders and saying to each other, "Oh, well, it doesn't matter which tank has the correct fuel because when it comes right down to it they're all the same, anyway"!

Many may ask me why I left Islam if I found it so fulfilling and satisfying. How could I think of causing the disruption in my family such as I knew would happen by changing my faith? Christianity is fine for Christians and Islam is fine for Muslims, so why didn't I just leave it at that?

The answer is that Christianity and Islam forced me to choose one or the other. I was faced with conflicting truth-claims. For the Quran and the Bible, the consequence of rejecting its message is to perish in one's sins, literally spending eternity in hell. That is why I could not simply shrug my shoulders and believe as I wished. I had to come to terms with what I had come to know of the teachings of Christ and the Bible.

"WHO DO MEN SAY I AM?"

"I am the way and the truth and the life," Jesus affirmed
categorically, "No one comes to the Father [God] except
through me" (John 14:6). Before one can decide whether
to accept or reject this statement, he must first come to
terms with the person of Christ. Who is Jesus that he could
make such an incredible claim?

While a Muslim, I had a very definite view as to who
Christ is, for my knowledge of him was based on the
authority of the Quran, which claims to be

> . . . a Book Sublime;
> falsehood comes not to it from before it
> nor from behind it; a sending down from
>   One All-wise, All-laudable. [Surah 41:41/42]

However, the Bible speaks of Jesus in an altogether
different light than that of the Quran.

Whatever may be said about the similarities between the
Jesus of the Quran and the Jesus of the Bible, there
are many striking differences—differences which make all
the difference in the world. To the Quran, Jesus "was
only the Messenger of God" (Surah 4:169/171). To the
Bible, Jesus is the "only Sovereign and Lord" (Jude 4),
who alone, as "king of kings and Lord of lords" (Rev.
19:16) is worthy of our utmost devotion and praise (Rev.
5:11-14).

It is easy to see the stark contrast between the Quranic
and biblical portrayals of Christ. In the Quran, it is stated:

> Truly, the likeness of
> Jesus, in God's sight,
> is as Adam's likeness;
> He created him of dust,
> then said He unto him,
> 'Be,' and he was. . . .
> This is the true story.
> There is no god but God . . . (Surah 3:52/59; 55/62).

In the Bible, Jesus declares, as no man ever did:

> My sheep listen to my voice; I know them, and they
> follow me. I give them eternal life, and they shall never
> perish; no one can snatch them out of my hand. My
> Father, who has given them to me, is greater than all;
> no one can snatch them out of my Father's hand. I and
> the Father are one (John 10:27-30).

The Jews, upon hearing these words of Christ, picked up
stones to stone him because he had claimed to be God
(v. 33). John would later write, "He is the true God and
eternal life" (1 John 5:20).

The character, the claims, and the miracles of Christ all
caused people to consider whether he was more than a
mere man. While crossing the Sea of Galilee, the disciples
of Jesus witnessed an extraordinary display of their Master's
power over nature. Caught in the midst of a fierce storm,
the disciples, fearing for their lives, exclaimed, "Lord, save
us! We're going to drown!" With a word Jesus rebuked the
wind and the raging waters and they became completely
calm. In utter astonishment, the disciples asked each other,
"What kind of man is this? Even the winds and the waves
obey him!" (Matt. 8:23-27).

Not only did Jesus display authority over the realm of
nature, he also exercised authority to forgive sins—clearly
validating his claim to deity. After Jesus told a paralytic
that his sins were forgiven, some of the religious leaders of
the day accused Jesus of blasphemy and rightly thought to
themselves, "Who can forgive sins but God alone?"
(Mark 2:7). But Jesus, knowing their hearts, posed the
question: "Which is easier to say, 'Your sins are forgiven,'
or to say, 'Get up and walk'?" His reasoning was obvious:
Only God could heal and only God could forgive. If Jesus
could heal the paralytic, this would verify his authority to
forgive sins. If he did not in fact have this authority,
God would not allow the healing. Therefore, Jesus went on

to say, " 'But so that you may know that the Son of Man
has authority on earth to forgive sins . . . .' Then he said to
the paralytic, 'Get up, take your mat and go home.' And
the man got up and went home" (Matt. 9:5-7).

Someone for whom miracles of love and grace were so
"natural" and plentiful was certain to be more than a mere
man. But Jesus was also to say many startling things
which indicated plainly his uniqueness among men. What
man ever said, as Christ did, "Whoever finds his life will
lose it, and whoever loses his life for My sake will find it"
(Matt. 10:39)? What man could claim to be "greater than
the temple," the very house of God (Matt. 12:6)? Or claim
to be "Lord of the Sabbath," the day set aside to be
consecrated to God (Matt. 12:8)?

Jesus was to question his disciples about his identity one
day as they traveled through Caesarea Philippi; but first
he would ask them,

" 'Who do people say the Son of Man is?' They replied,
'Some say John the Baptist; others say Elijah; and still
others, Jeremiah or one of the prophets.' 'But what about
you?' he asked. 'Who do you say I am?' Simon Peter
answered, 'You are the Christ [Messiah],[1] the Son of the
living God.' Jesus replied, 'Blessed are you, Simon son of
Jonah, for this was not revealed to you by man, but by
my Father in heaven.' " [Matthew 16:13-16]

The masses saw Jesus as one of the prophets returned
from the dead—a great man of God, but nevertheless a
mortal human being. Peter, however, by God's revelation,
had an entirely different insight. In his stirring declaration
we see Jesus as both "Messiah" and "Son," thus unfolding
for us the uniqueness of Christ's mission and nature. The
Quran, although attributing to Jesus the title of Messiah,
does not elaborate on any specific mission which the biblical
usage of the term implies. (Jesus, as the Messiah, is the
Anointed One, the Deliverer, the Savior.) More important,

as we have already seen in regard to the nature of Christ, the Quran explicitly rejects any concept of divine sonship. This brings us to the heart of our present discussion: What are we to make of the "Sonship" of Jesus, who is called Messiah (Christ) by both Quran and Bible?

THE SON OF GOD

Regarding Christ, the Quran understands sonship in terms of physical procreation. God "has not begotten, and has not been begotten . . ." (Surah 112).

> It is not for God to take a son
> unto Him. Glory be to Him! When He
> decrees a thing, He but says to it
>   "Be," and it is. [Surah 19:36/35]

When the Quran says that God does not "take a son unto him" it means that "God does not 'take to himself' or acquire offspring, in the manner of pagan deities."[2] With this it must be emphatically stated that the Bible is in complete agreement with the Quran.

However, the Quran denounces the biblical concept of the Son of God as sharply as it does the pagan belief in many gods:

> The Jews say, "Ezra is the Son of God";
> the Christians say, "the Messiah is the Son of God."
> That is the utterance of their mouths, conforming
> with the unbelievers before them. God assail them!
>   How they are perverted! [Surah 9:30]

Nowhere does the Bible teach that God had a son in "the manner of pagan deities" as the Quran supposes that Christians believe.

How, then, is Christ's Sonship understood in the Bible? If the Bible, by implication, rejects the concept of divine offspring as firmly as the Quran, it must have a very different view of Christ's Sonship than Muslims are led to believe. Why is it that the Quran's understanding is the wrong one?

In order to fully understand the term "Son of God," it is essential to see it in light of its Old Testament idiom. In the vast majority of cases, the Hebrew word "son" is used in the Old Testament in the normal sense of offspring or physical progeny. But the word is also used a significant number of times to denote a person's profession, condition or circumstance, character, or nature.[3] For instance, regarding one's profession, Zechariah 4:14 refers to "sons of fresh oil" (NASB), indicating anointed members of the priestly office. Second Chronicles 25:13 speaks of "sons of the troops" (NASB), simply meaning soldiers. In terms of one's condition or circumstance, Proverbs 31:5 calls people suffering affliction "sons of affliction" (NASB). The exiled Jews who had returned to their homeland were called "sons of exile" (Hebrew text), meaning, as it is usually translated, "exiles." "Son of valor" in 1 Samuel 14:52 is a man of valiant character. These passages all show that the idiom "son of" is used not only to refer to one's father, but also to one's profession, condition or circumstance, or to a certain character quality.

This idiom is also used several times to indicate a person's essential nature. Psalm 8:4 asks, "What is man that you are mindful of him, the son of man that you care for him?" In the commonly used Hebrew poetical device, the second phrase repeats the same thought as the first. When the psalmist here speaks of "man" and "son of man" he is talking about exactly the same thing, namely, that being who by his very nature is man. The term "son of man" in Job 16:21 is generally translated as just "man." About ninety times God addresses Ezekiel as "son of man," undoubtedly to emphasize Ezekiel's human nature as opposed to God's.

The language of the New Testament, being greatly influenced by the Old Testament, also uses "son" in the

same sense of meaning one's nature. Consider the
following examples: Jesus called James and John "Sons of
Thunder," evidently due to something thunderous about
their nature (Mark 3:17). A companion of the apostles
named Joseph was called Barnabas, which means "Son of
Encouragement" (Acts 4:36). He was called this not
because his father's name was Encouragement, but
because he was characterized as an encouraging person.
Paul speaks of "the sons of disobedience" in Ephesians
5:6 (NASB), referring to those people who are, by their
very nature, disobedient. It should be amply clear that
when the Bible uses the term, "son of," it often uses it in
the idiomatic sense of indicating nature or essence and
not origin or birth.

The Jews of Christ's day knew perfectly well that "when
Jesus said he was the Son of God, he was claiming to be
of the nature of God and equal with God.[4] "For this reason
the Jews tried all the harder to kill him; not only was
he breaking the Sabbath, but he was even calling God his
own Father, making himself equal with God" (John 5:18).

It is on this basis that Jesus could say, "The Father
judges no one, but has entrusted all judgment to the Son,
that all may honor the Son, just as they honor the Father.
He who does not honor the Son does not honor the Father,
who sent him" (John 5:22, 23).

There was no need for Jesus to state flatly, "I am God."
To say the least, this would have been an extremely
awkward thing for him to say in the culture in which he
lived. He would have been stoned immediately on the
grounds of blasphemy. In fact, he was ultimately executed
on the cross "because he claimed to be the Son of God"
(John 19:7), thus making himself out to be God. Also,
Jesus, although "being in very nature God, did not consider
equality with God something to be grasped" (Phil. 2:6). He
was not at all interested in flaunting his divine prerogatives.
It wasn't his way.

BEGOTTEN

Another term which was unclear to me as a Muslim was the word "begotten." In reference to Christ, this word is especially ambiguous since it implies a beginning or birth which the original Greek word need not, and undoubtedly does not, mean. "Begotten" is an old translation of the Greek word *monogenēs,* which is composed of the two words, *monos* (single) and *genos* (kind). We get our English word genus (meaning kind; sort; class) from *genos.* *Monogenēs* literally means "one of a kind" or "one and only." It is perhaps best translated as "unique."[5] Jesus is the unique Son of God. He is one of a kind. He is unique because he has a special relationship with the Father. While he is truly human, he is at the same time truly divine. And he shares his divine nature with the Father and the Holy Spirit.

THE TRINITY

The Bible, like the Quran, affirms the existence of only one God, yet it reveals a God who is at once Father, Son, and Spirit. Each of these names is a designation for one of the three persons who together comprise the unity of the Being of God. "Person" is not to be confused with human persons, but is used to indicate the distinctness and uniqueness of the Father, Son, and Holy Spirit. These three are not to be understood as three different manifestations of the same God. Each has his own individuality—each is separate from the others.

Therefore, the Father can love and communicate with the Son, and the Son with the Spirit, and the Spirit with the Father. God is not a solitary Being. From eternity past, before the creation of angels and man, a reciprocal relationship of love and communication existed among the members of the Trinity. There was no need for God to create anything, as if he needed the love and obedience and devotion of men and angels. No—he was complete in himself; he had all the love and fellowship needed for the fulfillment of a personal being.

But the Father, Son, and Holy Spirit are united in such a way that there is only one God. There are not three gods. Christians have never believed this. Therefore, when the Quran says, "They are unbelievers who say, 'God is the Third of Three.' No God is there but One God" (Surah 5:76/73), the Bible and the Christian agree.

What the Bible reveals is the tri-*unity* of God. And both Muslims and Christians will agree that what God reveals does not and cannot violate human reason, though it may certainly transcend our finite understanding. In the mystery of God's own Being, known only to himself, God is plurality within unity and unity around plurality. Although we are not able to comprehend fully the dynamics of the Trinity, neither are we able to comprehend even the most basic conception of God.

Some deny the Trinity on the basis that it cannot be understood, but can such people exhaustively understand their own view of God as an infinite, spiritual Being—a Being, that is, that cannot be seen, heard, or touched? To declare assertively that God cannot be a triune Being is really the height of arrogance. Who are we—as finite creatures, very limited in our understanding—to say what God can or cannot be? We are dependent on God for knowledge about himself. In nature, the higher form of a creature is always more complex than the lower forms, so when we consider God, who is the highest Being, does it not stand to reason that his Being is also the most complex? We know that God is a Trinity because he has revealed this to us.

This brings us to one of the fundamental points of divergence between Christianity and Islam—the way each believes God has revealed himself. This is crucial because both Muslims and Christians desire to worship God in the right way. In order to do so, however, we need to understand God in the right way and we need some kind of guarantee that we understand him in the right way.

Muslims believe that God has sent down to prophets throughout human history various books revealing truths to man about God and the world. Christians likewise believe that God has given man a written revelation of himself, the Books of the Old and New Testaments. This revelation was not "sent down" by God, but given through human authors under the guidance and inspiration of the Holy Spirit. However, the Bible declares that God not only *told* about himself, He also *showed* himself. God's word to man came not only as a written word, but also as the living Word. "The Word became flesh and lived for awhile among us. We have seen his glory, the glory of the one and only Son, who came from the Father, full of grace and truth" (John 1:14). "No one has ever seen God, but God the only Son, who is at the Father's side, has made him known" (John 1:18). God became man: he became one of us! "God was manifest in the flesh" (1 Tim. 3:16, KJV)—this is God's supreme revelation.

Now we can be sure that we truly know who God is and what he is like. This is our guarantee that we can understand God in the right way and therefore worship him in the right way. The Bible tells us that "in the past God spoke to our forefathers through the prophets at many times and in various ways, but in these last days he has spoken to us by his Son, whom he appointed heir of all things, and through whom he made the universe" (Heb. 1:1, 2). The Son is contrasted with the prophets, because he, unlike the mortal prophets before him, "is the radiance of God's glory and the exact representation of his being, sustaining all things by his powerful word" (v. 3). An old Christian man who had been a Muslim understood this very well when he said, "O Abd al Masih, every prophet is like the moon which shines in the darkness of this world. A prophet will be born like the new moon, and he will increase in size and power until he is like the full moon, then he will decrease and die. But do not worry. God will not leave the

world in darkness, for another moon will be born. That is
like the prophets; they were sent one after the other. A
prophet came, gave his message, and died. But look at that
sun, Abd al Masih, and tell me if it is the same sun as
you have in your country. Have you ever seen it decrease in
size or strength? Jesus said, 'I am the light of the world.'
He is like the sun. He is for all mankind, for every race,
and He will never decrease or die. Abd al Masih, look up
into the sky. Can you see the moon? Of course not, for the
sun is shining and who needs the moon when the sun has
come?"[6]

The Bible goes on to tell us that "after [Jesus] had
provided purification for sins, he sat down at the right hand
of the Majesty in heaven" (Heb. 1:3). Here we see that
Christ came not only to *reveal* God to man, but to *redeem*
man to God.

LIFE AND DEATH

When God created man, he created him in his own image
as a personal being. On this basis man was able to have a
relationship of free and open fellowship with God his
Creator. Love and communication existed between God
and man in a way that was not possible for all other
creatures, except angels. But with this tremendous privilege
came an equally awesome responsibility—man must not
violate the holiness and purity of God's own character.
Having been created with the capacity for choice, man in
time was required to choose between loyalty and rebellion.
In a willful act of disobedience, he chose the latter and
his intimate relationship with God was broken.

Not only was mankind estranged from God, but it has
since been plagued by a spiritual disease called sin. This
"sickness" has brought about a corruption in man's
nature—a corruption which, in God's eyes, has resulted in
a state of spiritual death. We do what we think brings life—
we "gratify the cravings of our sinful nature" and follow

"its desires and thoughts" (Eph. 2:3)—but such things cannot bring life because they are opposed to Christ, who is "the life" (John 14:6). Consequently, man is dead, even while he lives. He is separated from God, the fount of all life.

Biblically, death always conveys the idea of "separateness." As we are dead physically when separated from our bodies, so we are dead spiritually when separated from God. Both forms of separatioin have come about because sin entered the world. This means that "death came to all men, because all sinned" (Rom. 5:12). Death is the direct result of sin. Had man never sinned, there would be no death. It is important to see this, for death is an abnormality in God's creation. We must not blame God for our miserable lot. Man is not now what God had originally created him to be. Even the physical world was drastically affected by sin (Rom. 8:20-22; Gen. 3:17, 18).

THE LAW OF GOD

The most serious effect of man's sin is the evil nature with which he has been condemned. This tendency to evil which pervades man's nature is brought to light most strikingly when contrasted with God's righteous law as revealed in the Bible—primarily the Ten Commandments. We fall so short of God's righteous standards that we are compelled to bow before him, pleading for mercy. This is a basic purpose of the law—to reveal to us our own sinfulness. "Therefore no one will be declared righteous in his sight by observing the law; rather, through the law we became conscious of sin" (Rom. 3:20). Thus the law is not meant, as many suppose, including Muslims, only to provide an objective standard of morality that we are expected to keep. It is presumed that we cannot keep it. It shows us the utter sinfulness of sin (Rom. 7:13) and, consequently, reveals our desperate need of the mercy and forgiveness of God.

Many think they are in good standing before God because they have not killed anyone or committed adultery, nor do they steal or lie, thus violating the Ten Commandments. But they ignore the last commandment—Thou shalt not covet—which deals with the intentions of the inner man, thus bringing all the other commandments into focus. God observes not merely our outward actions. He "judges the thoughts and attitudes of the heart" (Heb. 4:12). Therefore, when we wrongly desire another's spouse or property, we are, in effect, committing adultery and stealing. When we hate someone we, in effect, commit murder. This is what makes (or should make) the Ten Commandments so terribly disturbing and condemning. And who, after all, has ever even remotely adhered to the commandment: "Love the Lord your God with all your heart and with all your soul and with all your mind and with all your strength" (Mark 12:30). We all are guilty of that idolatrous exultation of *self*. "Arrogance [is] like the evil of idolatry" (1 Sam. 15:23).

CONDEMNATION AND ETERNAL LIFE
The God of the Bible is an infinite, personal God whose being and character are the ground of all that exists. Because he is personal, God is a moral being, and his character is the standard by which all created personal beings must conform. Since God is infinite and unchanging, his character, including his attributes of love and justice, is absolute and perfect. Therefore, if God is to be just, all that goes on in his universe by any moral creature that violates his righteous standards must result in separation and banishment from him. For God cannot condone or tolerate any form of unrighteousness. Perhaps this is similar to a man whose honor has been defamed unjustly. The man feels compelled to vindicate his honor. He cannot passively accept the injustice that has been done to him.

God must condemn sin to vindicate his righteousness, otherwise he would be compromising his own righteous character. As God is infinite, any sin against his character carries infinite consequences. If one is to bear these consequences he must experience eternal separation from God, which, in the Bible, is called the "second death" (Rev. 20:14). Because we lack a firm sense of justice, we think it unfair that God should deal so harshly with sin. However, we can understand the consequences of sin only if we fully appreciate the intrinsic holiness of God. This we cannot do because we are blinded by our own sinfulness to the true nature of good and evil. Only when the prophet Isaiah "saw the Lord seated on a throne, high and exalted," did he cry out, "Woe to me! I am ruined! For I am a man of unclean lips, and I live among a people of unclean lips, and my eyes have seen the King, the Lord Almighty" (Isaiah 6:1, 5).

If the law was given "so that every mouth may be silenced and the whole world held accountable to God" (Rom. 3:19), the question naturally arises, "Is there any hope?" Is there any way to be rescued from our terrible plight, for, as the law shows us, if God is just, he owes us nothing but judgment, "because law brings wrath" (Rom. 4:15)?

LOVE AND JUSTICE

The Bible assures us that "God is Love" (1 John 4:8). He abounds in mercy. His love automatically opposes condemnation. It is not his desire to punish anyone. Yet he cannot arbitrarily forgive sin. If a judge acquits a criminal, the judge is being unjust and is himself evil. The criminal must be sentenced for punishment. While love demands that sin be forgiven, justice demands that sin be punished.

If a person is to be reconciled to God and forgiven of his sin, he must himself pay the penalty for his sin. No one can do this, for simply no one can pay a penalty of eternal value except by spending eternity apart from God, which means, of course, no reconciliation. Unless some provision

is made for the penalty of sin, thereby allowing for the
removal of guilt, forgiveness cannot be granted. A creation
which required God to create cannot be redeemed by one
less than God. Thus, if there is to be any salvation for man,
it must originate from God, for God himself must pay the
penalty. He is the only one able to do so for only he is
infinite.

However, God cannot punish himself in the form of God
as this would not relate to man, because man is the sinner.
So God became man at a point in time in human history
to take upon himself the due penalty of mankind's sin. God
came into the world in the person of his Son who took on
human flesh in the womb of the virgin Mary. "In the
beginning was the Word, and the Word was with God, and
the Word was God . . . The Word became flesh and lived
for awhile among us" (John 1:1, 14). As the Messiah, the
Deliverer, Jesus became a man to represent mankind
before God. Adam, the first man, represented the human
race before God, but the result of his one act of
disobedience "was condemnation for all men." "The
result of one act of righteousness" by the last Adam, Jesus
Christ (1 Cor. 15:45), "was justification that brings life for
all men" (Rom. 5:18).

This "one act of righteousness" was Christ's "sacrifice of
atonement" whereby he satisfied God's just demands for
judgment on sin by his death on the cross. Christ died as
our substitute by bearing for us on the cross God's wrath
against sin so that we might not undergo this same
judgment. Read carefully these words of the Apostle Paul:

> But now a righteousness from God, apart from law, has
> been made known, to which the Law and the Prophets
> testify. This righteousness from God comes through faith
> in Jesus Christ to all who believe. There is no difference,
> for all have sinned and fall short of the glory of God,
> and are justified freely by his grace through the
> redemption that came by Christ Jesus. God presented

him as a sacrifice of atonement, through faith in his blood. He did this to demonstrate his justice, because in his forbearance he had left the sins committed beforehand unpunished—he did it *to demonstrate his justice* at the present time, so as to be just and the one who justifies the man who has faith in Jesus (Romans 3:21-26, italics mine) . . . . But God *demonstrates his own love* for us in this: While we were still sinners, Christ died for us (Romans 5:8, italics mine).

Nowhere in the Quran or the traditions of Islam does Allah demonstrate his love for mankind; that is, a love that gives of itself—a self-sacrificing love. God's love in the Quran is like a businessman's love.[7] He will love those who meet his conditions, but those who are at enmity with him he will not love. The God of the Bible, on the other hand, displays a love that transcends the love experienced in human relationships. Is it worthy of God that his love should be on the level of man? How could God not have a love that is higher than man's love? God's love reaches out even to his enemies (Rom. 5:10). He is the One who always initiates a relationship of love between himself and a man or woman.

This is how God showed his love among us: He sent his one and only Son into the world that we might live through him. This is love: not that we loved God, but that he loved us and sent his Son as an atoning sacrifice for our sins. (1 John 4:9, 10).

"At the very heart of God's sovereignty is sacrificial and suffering love."[8]

We see in the cross of Christ the meeting of the love and justice of the sovereign, holy God. His demand for justice is satisfied in that he inflicted the due penalty of sin upon himself in the person of his Son. His demand for love is satisfied in that he provides a way for the sinner to be forgiven and not have to be punished for his sin. God can declare a guilty man righteous and remain righteous himself. He remains forever just and forever loving. Islam has no way to reconcile the love and justice of God in relation to sinful man.

In the cross we also see the seriousness of sin, for we see the extent to which God had to go to atone for it. The tragedy of man's rebellion against God caused the Father to punish the Son on our behalf. We see mystery here—the mystery and glory that is God himself. We must be careful not to insist that God fit neatly into our own dimension of human understanding. Do we dare claim the capacity to completely comprehend the infinite God? Let us be awed at the beauty and magnitude of this drama of redemption as revealed in the Bible. And let us worship the Incarnate God who has given himself for us and invites us to come to him for life eternal.

JUSTIFICATION

A good definition and illustration of justification has been given by Francis Schaeffer.

> Justification is the declaration on God's part that we are just in his sight because he has imputed to us the obedience of Christ. This means that God charges our sins to Christ's account. He attributes to us the obedience of Christ. It is as if a little child enters a store and buys more than he can pay for. Then the parent arrives and says, "Charge that to my account." The child's debt is erased. The parent pays. When we are justified, God charges the punishment due to the guilt of our sin to the account of Christ.[9]

The means by which the righteousness of Christ becomes ours is by faith apart from any religious or moral good works. Faith alone has always been the way of salvation.

The Apostle Paul proves this historically by citing the examples of Abraham and David. David spoke of "the blessedness of the man to whom God credits righteousness apart from works" (Rom. 4:6) and "Abraham believed God, and it was credited to him as righteousness" (Rom. 4:3). "The words 'it was credited to him' were written not for him alone, but also for us, to whom God will credit righteousness—for us who believe in him who raised Jesus our Lord from the dead" (Rom. 4:23, 24).

The means to salvation is the fundamental difference between Islam and Christianity. The faithful Muslim will do his best to keep the five pillars of his faith, thinking that by so doing he will be more likely to win God's favor. The five pillars are: 1) the often repeated confession, "There is no god but God; Mohammed is the apostle of God," 2) the five daily ritual prayers, 3) keeping the Fast of Ramadan, 4) the giving to the poor of 2-1/2 percent of one's income, 5) making the pilgrimage to Mecca at least once during one's lifetime if it is financially possible. The sensitive Muslim will constantly be under tension while he awaits his future fate, because, although he continually strives to do his best for God, God may or may not forgive him on the Last Day. Faith is essential for the Muslim as well as the Christian, but the stress is on intellectual belief and not trust in God as the One in whom faith rests.

The Bible teaches that it is only by faith in Christ that a person can be forgiven of his sins.

> What is faith in Christ? A missionary when seeking a native word for faith could not find it. Finally, he sat in a chair and raised his feet from the ground, putting his full weight on the chair and bearing none of his weight himself. He then asked what word described his act, and used that word for faith. This is an accurate picture. Faith in Christ is resting totally on him and his finished work.[10]

God wants us to place our total confidence in him. Since we are not able to save ourselves God offers forgiveness to us as a gift. He will not force himself upon us because he has given us the right to accept or reject him. As all gifts are free and must be received, so also if we are to be saved we must respond to God's offer and take what Christ died to give us. When we do, God will not only declare us righteous in his sight, but he will impart to us new life— the life of his Spirit who will come into us and transform our inner being. The Holy Spirit will enable us to increasingly conform our lives to the image of Christ so that we will be like him in all our thoughts and actions.

Because I have asked Christ into my life, confessing my sin and receiving his gift of forgiveness, God has given me complete and total assurance that I stand forgiven before him. If I were to die at any moment, I am assured of eternal life with my matchless Savior whom I love more than all else. I have no fear of being forever separated from God, for the blood of Christ has made me whole. In Christ, I am "a new creation; the old has gone, the new has come!" (2 Cor. 5:17). I have come to know God in all his fullness, for I know the Father who loves me, the Son who saves me, and the Holy Spirit who resides within me. To experience God is, in the words of the Apostle Paul, to experience "the grace of the Lord Jesus Christ, and the love of God [the Father], and the fellowship of the Holy Spirit" (2 Cor. 13:14).

NOTES

Preface

[1]See *The Ventura County (Calif.) Star-Free Press,* 4 November 1979 and "Newsmakers," *Newsweek,* June 16, 1980, p. 97.

[2]*The Ventura County (Calif.) Star-Free Press,* 4 November 1979, p. A-14.

Chapter 1

[1]The Arabic word "Allah" is the same in meaning as the English word "God." Both denote the Supreme Being. Strictly speaking, "Allah" is not to be taken as a certain concept of God as distinguished from another, although Christians and Muslims do differ in their views of God.

Chapter 3

[1]President for Life was a title he assumed in August 1976.

[2]Henry Kyemba, *A State of Blood* (New York: Paddington Press, 1977), p. 15.

Chapter 4

[1]Dave Toycen, "Ugandan Christians: The Horror and the Hope," *World Vision,* July, 1979, p. 9.

[2]Henry Kyemba, *A State of Blood* (New York: Paddington Press, 1977), p. 248.

[3]Festo Kivengere, *I Love Idi Amin* (Old Tappan, N.J.: Revell, 1977), p. 30.

[4]"Threnody for the Rebels," *Time,* April 8, 1974, p. 40.

[5]"God Help the People," *Time,* September 25, 1972, pp. 32-33.

[6]"Big Daddy's Big Mouth," *Time,* September 17, 1973, p. 47.

[7]Stanley Meisler, "Uganda," *The Atlantic,* December, 1972, p. 37.

Chapter 5

[1]"Black Racism in Uganda—White Man's Burden for Britain," *U.S. News & World Report,* September 4, 1972, p. 49.

Chapter 8

[1]In the Quran, when Allah speaks the pronoun "we" is used instead of "I."

[2]Geoffrey Parrinder, *Jesus in the Quran* (New York: Oxford University Press, 1977), p. 145.

³Although I would hold this to be true of Muslims generally, it must be noted that not all are of this opinion. Some Muslims believe the text has been misinterpreted, not tampered with. See Geoffrey Parrinder, *Jesus* in the Quran (New York: Oxford University Press, 1977), pp. 145-147).

⁴In Surah 2: 41/44 the Quran says, "Will you bid/others to piety, and forget yourselves/while you recite the Book? Do you not understand?" If the Quran blames the people of the Book for not living according to the teachings of the Scriptures which they read [the Bible] it must regard that text as correct.

⁵Despite the sad statements in Surah 5:56, 62/51, 57 these are not the last word in the matter. They are qualified by Surah 5:73/69 and by the passage quoted in the next sentence.

Chapter 9

¹When I became a Christian, I wrote to Dr. Graham asking forgiveness for my rudeness. He was gracious enough to later contact me and inform me that he had received my letter. Not only did he forgive me, but he also asked forgiveness from me (as if he had to!) for not responding immediately to what I said while I was in the crowd.

Chapter 10

¹I am not denying the need for faith, but only stressing here that Islam does not require the transformation, or regeneration, of one's inner being by God himself.

²Geoffrey Parrinder, *Jesus in the Quran* (New York: Oxford University Press, 1977), p. 58.

³*Ibid.*, pp. 134-136.

⁴Although it is true that I used an Arabic Quran which I could not understand, I did have a basic knowledge and understanding of Islam which I gained through formal religious education and the reading of books about my faith.

⁵See Surahs 3:29/31-32; 2:191/195; and 2:222 respectively.

Chapter 14

¹The Greek word for *Christ* means the same as the Hebrew word for *Messiah.* Both mean "the Anointed One."

²Geoffrey Parrinder, *Jesus in the Quran* (New York: Oxford University Press, 1977), p. 80.

³My discussion of the idiomatic use of "son" in the Bible is based on a paper by S. Herbert Bess of Grace Theological Seminary, "The Term 'Son of God' in the Light of Old Testament Idiom." (Mimeographed.)

⁴*Ibid.*, p. 3.

⁵The meaning of *monogenēs* is further clarified by its use in Hebrews 11:17 where it is used of Isaac, Abraham's son. Isaac was certainly not Abraham's only begotten son, because Abraham had several other children (Genesis 25:2). Isaac as *monogenēs* was the unique (only) son of the Promise. Jesus as *monogenēs* was the unique (only) Son of God. Jesus' relationship with the Father was unique.

⁶Charles R. Marsh, *Share Your Faith With a Muslim* (Chicago: Moody Press, 1975), p. 36.

⁷See Charles Cutler Torrey, *The Commercial Theological Terms in the Koran* (Leyden: E. J. Brill, 1892).

⁸H. D. McDonald, *Jesus—Human and Divine* (Grand Rapids, Michigan: Zondervan Publishing House, 1968), p. 69.

⁹Francis A. Schaeffer, *Basic Bible Studies* (Wheaton, Illinois: Tyndale House Publishers, 1972), p. 52.

¹⁰*Ibid.*, p. 53.

SUGGESTED READING

Arberry, Arthur J. *The Koran Interpreted.* New York: Macmillan, 1964.
A very readable, yet scholarly, English translation which attempts to retain the poetic spirit and style of the Quran in Arabic.

Clark, Dennis E. *The Life and Teaching of Jesus the Messiah (Sirat-ul-Masih, Isa, Ibn Maryam).* Elgin: Dove Publications, 1977.
Written with Muslim readers in mind. It is available in several languages of the Muslim world, including Arabic.

Elder, John. *The Biblical Approach to the Muslim.* Houston: LIT International.
An excellent study for Christian workers.

Hanna, Mark. *The True Path, Seven Muslims Make their Greatest Discovery.* Colorado Springs: International Doorways Publications, 1975.
Presents seven testimonies by Muslims of varying backgrounds who have come to christ. Contains an extensive glossary of Christian terms, plus a chapter explaining the Biblical way of salvation.

Jomier, Jacques. *The Bible and the Koran.* New York: Desclee Company, 1964.

Jones, L. Bevan. *Christianity Explained to Muslims, A Manual for Christian Workers.* Revised edition. Calcutta: YMCA Publishing House, 1952.
Another excellent study for Christian workers.

Kivengere, Festo. *I Love Idi Amin.* Old Tappan, N.J.: Revell, 1977.

Kyemba, Henry. *A State of Blood.* New York: Paddington Press, 1977.

Marsh, Charles R. *Share Your Faith With a Muslim.* Chicago: Moody Press, 1975.
A good introduction for those unacquainted with Islam.

Miller, William M. *A Christian's Response to Islam.* Wheaton, Il: Tyndale House Publishers, Inc., 1980.

―――――――――. *Ten Muslims Meet Christ.* Grand Rapids: Eerdmans, 1969.

Parrinder, Geoffrey. *Jesus in the Qur'an.* New York: Oxford University Press, 1977.
Written for both Christians and Muslims.

Pickthall, Muhammad M. *The Meaning of the Glorious Qur'an.* New York: Dover Publications, 1977.
An explanatory translation by a British Muslim. This is perhaps the best version for christians to use in dialogue with Muslims. A handsome hardbound copy is obtainable free of charge by writing to The Muslim World League, U.N. Office; 300 East 44th Street, New York, N.Y. 10017.

Smith, Wilfred Cantwell. *Islam in Modern History.* Princeton: Princeton University press, 1957.
A more advanced study written for both the scholar and the general reader.

Wilson, J. Christy. *Introducing Islam.* New York: Friendship Press, 1959.

Wooding, Dan and Barnett, Ray. *Uganda Holocaust.* Grand Rapids: Zondervan Publishing House, 1980.

Your Muslim Guest, A Practical Guide in Friendship and Witness for Christians Who Meet Muslims in North America. Toronto: Fellowship of Faith for Muslims, 1976.

My recommendation of these books, of course, is in no way to be understood as an endorsement of all that they contain.

Anyone interested in obtaining more information pertaining to a Christian witness to Muslims may write to the following:

The Samuel Zwemer Institute
Box 365
Altadera, CA 91001
(213) 794-1121/1122

Fellowship of Faith for the Muslims
205 Yonge Street
Toronto, Ontario, Canada
M5B 1N2